Coming to Grips with
Huckleberry Finn

Coming to Grips with
Huckleberry Finn

Essays on a Book, a Boy, and a Man

Tom Quirk

University of Missouri Press
Columbia and London

Library of Congress Cataloging-in-Publication Data

Quirk, Tom, 1946–
    Coming to grips with Huckleberry Finn : essays on a
book, a boy, and a man / Tom Quirk.
        p.   cm.
    Includes index.
    ISBN 0–8262–0920–3
    1. Twain, Mark, 1835–1910. Huckleberry Finn. 2. Boys in
literature. I. Title.
PS1305.Q57   1993
813'.4—dc20   93–25042
                                                           CIP

∞ This paper meets the requirements of the
American National Standard for Permanence of Paper
for Printed Library Materials, Z39.48, 1984.

Designer: Kristie Lee
Typesetter: Connell-Zeko Type & Graphics
Printer and Binder: Thomson-Shore, Inc.
Typeface: Schneidler

For George W. Arms (1912–1992)
and Louis J. Budd

Two peas in a pod

Contents

Acknowledgments

M OST OF THESE ESSAYS have been or will be published else-where, and all are reprinted by permission. "Life Imitating Art: *Huckleberry Finn* and Twain's Autobiographical Writings" ap-peared in *One Hundred Years of "Huckleberry Finn": The Boy, His Book, and American Culture; Centennial Essays,* ed. Robert Sattelmeyer and J. Donald Crowley (Columbia: University of Missouri Press, 1985). "'Learning a Nigger to Argue': Quitting *Huckleberry Finn*" was pub-lished in *American Literary Realism* (Fall 1987). "Nobility out of Tatters: The Writing of *Huckleberry Finn*" appeared in *Writing the American Classics,* ed. James Barbour and Tom Quirk (Chapel Hill: University of North Carolina Press, 1990). "The Realism of *Huckleberry Finn,*" in a somewhat shorter version and under the title *"Adventures of Huckle-berry Finn,"* will appear in the *Cambridge Companion to American Real-ism and Naturalism,* ed. Donald Pizer (forthcoming, Cambridge: Cam-bridge University Press). "Is *Huckleberry Finn* Politically Correct?" in somewhat different form will appear as a part of a collection on *Realism and the Canon: A Collection of Essays,* ed. Gary Scharnhorst and Tom Quirk (forthcoming, Newark: University of Delaware Press). "Huckleberry Finn's Heirs" was prepared for this volume.

This book is dedicated to two men who, for me, represent all that is right with the professional study of literature. George Arms was, and Louis Budd is, better than I am, better scholars and critics, of course, but better men as well. I forgive them their advantages.

I learned a great deal from George Arms and Louis Budd, but I have learned from and been helped by others as well. Howard Baetzhold, Richard Barksdale, J. Donald Crowley, Leon Dickinson, Victor Doyno, Victor Fischer, Alan Gribben, Susan Harris, Hamlin Hill, Jervis Langdon, Robert Sattelmeyer, David Smith, Thomas Tenney—they, and so many others, contributed something to my thinking about Twain and his book, whether they know it or not. All of these people may well refuse the arguments and conclusions of my essays, but I hope they will accept this note of gratitude nonetheless. A final note of thanks must go to my wife and daughters. They humored me.

Coming to Grips with
Huckleberry Finn

Introduction

ONLY ONCE, AND THEN only for a moment, did I ever feel that I really knew how Mark Twain's imagination worked. I was in my car, stopped at a red light. Directly across from me a squirrel was running nicely between the white lines of the pedestrian crosswalk. The squirrel was about halfway across when the light changed from green to yellow. At that same instant, the squirrel screeched to a halt and ran back the way he had come. Alone in the car and without thinking, I shouted, "You, idiot! You could have made it!" I sometimes believe that that was how Twain saw the world—quite literally as an intersection: an intersection of the natural and the mechanical (Bergson's familiar theory of comedy). An intersection, too, of the spontaneous remark that recoils upon the speaker—for who is the idiot after all but the man who chides squirrels, an essentially upright citizen who wouldn't think of crossing at a red light, but who observes the letter not the spirit of the law and spontaneously thinks that squirrels ought to know better than to be so scrupulous when there are no cops in sight.

I cite this anecdote as a way of admitting that Mark Twain remains something of a mystery to me. The essays gathered together here were written over a several year period, and many have been published before. They represent repeated attempts to come to grips with Twain's most provocative and enchanted novel, *Adventures of Huckleberry Finn*. What my efforts prove, I suspect, is that I have always come up short. I can say in their defense, however, that I have gone at Twain's novel from a number of angles, and I summarize them here in the order in which they appear in this volume: I have inquired into the genesis and composition of the book; I have tried to measure the author's imaginative involvement with his young hero by studying the novel in the context of Twain's autobiographical writings; I have speculated on the compositional, as opposed to the narrative, conclusion of the novel as a way of throwing certain cross-lights on the vexed question of the evasion episode; I have examined the special and curious relation *Huckleberry Finn* bears to nineteenth-century American realism; I have contemplated a double legacy Twain and his novel have bequeathed to later American writers; and, finally, I have, in rather antic fashion, measured the book against current ideological opinion.

The reason for the arrangement of the essays as they appear in this collection is that, collectively, they follow a broad chronological pattern—from the inception of the book through its several stages of composition, on to the special quality of its literary realism, and at last to the influence the novel has had upon subsequent generations of readers and writers. Historically considered, one might say that the essays move from that day in 1876 at Quarry Farm when Twain began his story of Huck's adventures to the moment only a few years ago when someone, somewhere, revived that unhappy phrase "political correctness." Considered in yet another way, one might say they comprise a very brief episode in the history of the imagination. For I am typically more interested in how this book came to be and why it has affected so many people for so long in so many curious ways than in how to interpret or to "read" the book. And because, fundamentally, I am more interested in the acts of the imagination than in interpretation or critical evaluation, I have tended to rely rather heavily upon the observations of other creative writers to clarify or extend my several arguments. In particular, I find now that I came back again and again to a handful of writers who speak eloquently on the mysteries of the imagination and the felt social and moral responsibilities of the artist—Wright Morris, Willa Cather, Ralph Ellison, and Wallace Stevens. Finally, considered generically, these essays are specimens of a familiar scholarly inquiry and humanistic criticism.

Of that dimension of the essays, I will have more to say in a moment.

In sum, over the years I have adapted my means to my ends. Those ends were, by and large, prompted by personal curiosity rather than by a desire to respond to long-standing and preestablished critical or theoretical issues. Whatever their deficiencies, the several essays confidently affirm by example that there are a good many ways to go at *Huckleberry Finn,* and by taking several of those available avenues of understanding I have tried to corral a number of the mysteries of the book. Actually, I am not so very confident in this approach. For I am reminded of Twain's remark to Dan De Quille: "Dan, there is more than one way of writing a book; & your way is not the right one."

And, in point of fact, circumstances have conspired against me, as well as a good many others, to demonstrate that on several matters I was unmistakably wrong. A few years ago, over 665 manuscript pages in Twain's neat hand were discovered in a trunk in California. They have been described as the "first half" of the *Huckleberry Finn* manuscript, though actually those pages, with cancellations and insertions, represent something less than half of the book. This new material includes an early version of chapters 1 through 21, but does not include part of chapter 12 and all of chapters 13 and 14, which were already extant in the previously known manuscript. The discovery of this lost portion of the manuscript, long thought to have been permanently lost, is both a joy and a damned nuisance. It is a joy because, now that it has come home to be reunited with the second half of the manuscript in the Buffalo and Erie County Public Library, we have a cultural treasure preserved in a public institution. The discovery is a nuisance because scholars and critics are now forced to abandon many cherished beliefs and settled opinions about how the book was composed.

It is too early to know how significantly these manuscript pages will alter our understanding, not of the book itself so much as of the author's struggles with and involvement in his narrative. Certainly they will provide a number of added clues to the strange workings of Twain's creative imagination, and the revisions and excisions may tell us more about how his literary ambitions and intentions changed over the seven-year period in which the novel was composed.

Before the discovery of the new manuscript material I wrote the following about Walter Blair's landmark studies of the composition of the novel:

> Blair's account of when *Huckleberry Finn* was written is so thoroughgoing and his conclusions so meticulously intelligent that for thirty years it has withstood the minute scrutiny of scholars and critics (including those involved in the Mark Twain Project specifically engaged in accumulating new evidence about the book). His conclusions about the stages of composition have remained pretty much intact and unchallenged.

For me, *Mark Twain and Huck Finn,* Blair's book-length genetic history of the novel, remains an admirable piece of work, as thorough and intelligent and stimulating as it ever was. However, on several points he was wrong. Facts are sometimes brutes and have a way of roughing up even the most carefully crafted hypotheses of the most responsible scholars.

Since many of the points I make in the essays having specifically to do with the composition of *Huckleberry Finn* are simply untrue, and since I have decided that perhaps it is better (and certainly more honest) to let the essays stand the way they were written instead of trying to repair the damage, I will summarize some of the things we have already learned from the newly discovered manuscript:

—It had long been assumed that the first phase of composition in 1876 ended at that part of chapter 16 where the riverboat runs over the raft. This is a very appealing notion because it invites us to imagine an author who didn't quite know how his narrative was developing. Huck and Jim had passed Cairo in the fog, and the author was in the absurd position of having a runaway slave escaping into the deep South. It would have been just like Twain to have gotten frustrated with this turn of events and, rather angrily one supposes, to have busted the raft all to flinders and to have pigeonholed the manuscript. The evidence reveals, however, that Twain's first stint of composition got him well beyond this point, to that part of chapter 18 where Buck Grangerford asks Huck, "Don't you know what a feud is?"[1]

—The most surprising revelation disclosed by the new evidence, perhaps, is that the so-called Hamlet soliloquy the duke teaches the king at the beginning of chapter 21 appears not to have been inserted into the chapter later. Though there may have been some interval between the creation of the dramatic situation for the recitation and the writing of the soliloquy itself, it evidently was planned as an integral part of the incident as it had originally been written, probably in 1879 or 1880.[2] This is surprising because other sorts of evidence Blair had come across in the Mark Twain Papers seemed clearly to indicate that it had been written in New York on that night probably in March 1883, when Clemens had refused to go to the opera with Livy and Charlie Webster and his wife. Again, the story conforms so nicely with what we know (or think we know) about Mark Twain that it is easy to picture this amusing mishmash of lines from Shakespeare as a typical act of Twainian mischief and a private triumph over efforts to civilize him.

—The manuscript discloses a few other notable surprises, as well. Though he evidently plotted his narrative according to episodes or adventures, Twain's chapter divisions in the manuscript do not correspond to those in the printed book. Also, he removed a grotesque episode about Huck and Jim wondering whether or not lightning casts a shadow followed by Jim recalling his adventures in fright

---

1. *Adventures of Huckleberry Finn,* vol. 8 of *The Works of Mark Twain,* ed. Walter Blair and Victor Fischer (Berkeley and Los Angeles: University of California Press [in cooperation with the University of Iowa], 1988), 146. Subsequent references to the novel will be to this edition and included parenthetically in the text.

2. Manuscript page 617 ends about halfway down the page with Huck's statement "This is the speech—I learned it, easy enough, while he was learning it to the king." The soliloquy begins at the top of 618 and runs into 622, where Huck's narrative is resumed. Since Twain did not typically take up a new sheet of paper when he was working and had space on the one before him, the implication is that there may have been some sort of break in the composition, but not one of any significant duration. On this point and other matters pertaining to the significance of the new manuscript, I am indebted to Victor Doyno.

while warming a cadaver for a young medical student. Finally, there are a few teasing changes in the title page and in the opening statement of the book. Originally, Twain had given his story the working title "Huckleberry Finn/Reported by Mark Twain," thus placing himself in a rather definite relation to his created character. And Huck's famous introduction of himself to the reader had at first been a good deal more proper and grammatical: "You will not know about me," Twain wrote; then he amended the opening statement to read "You do not know me" before he settled on the familiar "You don't know about me without you have read. . . ."

Had a complete manuscript been available at the time I wrote the first three essays in this volume (along with the commentary and conclusions of scholars such as Walter Blair who are more patient, competent, and intelligent than I am in deciphering all the implications that the discovered pages will one day reveal), I am sure that I would have written the pieces somewhat differently. I am not certain, however, that I would have reached dramatically different sorts of conclusions. Our perceptions continually outdistance our facts. To a degree, interpretation is always restrained by fact. Scholarship regulates and often formalizes humanistic inquiry; it keeps analysis and interpretation within the rules of evidence and the bounds of permissible inference. But a change in what is known about a given subject does not automatically invalidate the inquiry itself or, in some rare instances, even disturb the value of its conclusions. In any event, what's done is done, and for better or worse I will stand by the substance of the pieces, while openly acknowledging their occasional factual errors.

Quite apart from the several implications and revelations that the newly discovered manuscript material may disclose, I ought to mention the scholarly and critical work of Victor Doyno, whose *Writing Huck Finn: Mark Twain's Creative Process* (Philadelphia: University of Pennsylvania Press, 1991) was published after I had said my say about compositional matters. Had it been available to me, however, I suspect that I would have filched from it the way I did from Walter Blair's *Mark Twain and Huck Finn* (Berkeley and Los Angeles: University of California Press, 1960). As it stands, it would be indecent of me to try to summarize Doyno's thorough genetic study of the novel. It is a fine and substantial complement to Blair's earlier study, and I simply recommend it to that considerable number of readers who are interested in the rich and problematic history of the novel and the equally rich and complicated imagination of the man who produced it.

An ingredient in that complex imagination is undoubtedly the moral indignation Twain so often felt and that sometimes motivated his fictions. The subjects of that indignation, it is true, were frequently his own trivial and petty annoyances. Nevertheless, if Twain had a genuine desire to keep himself morally "clean," and sometimes altered the facts of his own experience to represent a more blameless life than he had actually lived, his complaints against the damned human race seldom, if ever, degenerated into simple self-righteousness. At odd moments, Twain turned his moral vision inward upon himself, and part of the interest of *Huckleberry Finn,* as a historical and biographical document, has to do with Clemens's own struggles with issues he sometimes raised but only imperfectly understood. Perhaps the most complex moral issue in the novel, certainly the most hotly debated question among literary critics and common readers today, has to do with problems of race and racial prejudice. If there are answers to this vexed question, they are to be found in Twain's mysterious involvement and identification with his created characters. As I have tried to show in some of the following essays, Twain's struggles on this score are located and epitomized in the character of Jim, not Huck—Jim both as a fictional creation and as a moral and political dilemma. Jim stirred Twain's imagination and piqued his normally troubled conscience, and, given the way that this runaway slave was unnecessarily complicating his narrative, any rational and less committed writer would have dumped him overboard at the first opportunity. But he did not. Instead, the evidence indicates that Twain worried over and worked hard in his rendering of Jim; he tried to imagine Jim's life, and he tried to give his character a living voice.

There is a dimension of Mark Twain that the so-called common reader has probably never lost sight of, though critics sometimes have. He was a moral man. I do not say he was an admirable man, or even a good man; and in the concluding essay I insist that, to speak idiomatically, if we "valorize" Twain's sensitivity, we will have lost much that is important about him. But Twain was a writer of strong imaginative sympathies and democratic convictions, and one troubled by a pained conscience. William Dean Howells knew him better than we do now, and he admired Twain's moral earnestness. Howells wrote the following remarks about Tolstoy, but he felt the same way about Twain: "You feel instantly that the man is mighty, and mighty through his conscience; that he is not trying to surprise or dazzle you with his art, but that he is trying to make you think clearly and feel rightly about vital things with which 'art' has often dealt with diabolical indifference or diabolical malevolence." Of course Twain's attempts to render the black experience are often as embarrassing and ridiculous as were Tolstoy's attempts to play the peasant. But that does not subtract from his effort to make us, as well as himself, feel rightly about vital things.

The reader will soon enough discover that the following essays are rather old-fashioned in their concerns. They are specimens of what used to be known as humanist inquiry—which is another way of saying that my convictions, my optimism, and my skepticism openly compete with one another; that my perceptions and interests are modified by and forever vulnerable to the dictates of an ever-changing fund of evidence; and that my conclusions are inevitably tentative and provisional. I suppose I ought to know better, but somehow I can't quite believe, as evidently so many critics and theorists do right now, that our most serious problems have all that much to do with problems of discourse. I wish I could believe that the world is a text, that our language thinks us, and so forth. If I could, I could also believe that literary performance and critical interpretation are hugely and urgently important political activities. But I can't, and they aren't. Imaginative literature is a rather small thing, after all; that is its distinction, not its liability.

I confess that I still believe in literary values (an old-fashioned conception in itself) and like to think they spill over into the realm of public and political life, the way I imagine the local pastor likes to believe his sermon will carry through till Monday. I like to think, along with Kenneth Burke, that imaginative literature supplies us with "equipment for living." And I suspect Willa Cather was right when she remarked that "Citizen Shelley," as she calls him, whatever the force of his political dogma, was finally more "useful" "only as all true poets are, because they refresh and recharge the spirit of those who can read their language." I like to believe, as well, that the imagination is not its own excuse, but a resource and an enlargement. And I want to believe, along with Wallace Stevens, that "the chief problems of any artist, as of any man, are the problems of the normal and that he needs, in order to solve them, everything that the imagination has to give." I want to believe all these things, and on good days I do. I really do. Sometimes, I locate those beliefs and that hope in the figure of a fourteen-year-old boy.

Huckleberry Finn made his literary debut in *The Adventures of Tom Sawyer*. He was wearing a baggy overcoat and swinging a dead cat. He claimed he had a cure for warts. Over the years I have come to believe, rightly or wrongly, that he has a cure for so much more. If only one could combine the squandered energies of youth with the bitter economies of experience, if only in the imagination one could meet Huck Finn at midnight by a spunk-water stump, I sometimes believe we might learn a cure for what ails us. Of course, this is only a superstition of mine.

NOBILITY OUT OF TATTERS
The Writing of *Huckleberry Finn*

I

WILLA CATHER ONCE WROTE, "There is a time in a writer's development when his 'life line' and the line of his personal endeavor meet." For her, the intersection of these two lines occurred when she wrote her first significant novel, *O Pioneers!* (1913). The writing of this novel produced in her the excitement that comes from writing out of one's "deepest experience" and "inner feeling," and her course was directed by the "thing by which our feet find the road on a dark night, accounting of themselves for roots and stones which we have never noticed by day."[1] These remarks are as true for Mark Twain as they were for Cather herself; and whether he knew it or not, the lines of his familiar experience and his literary ambition converged sometime in July 1876, when he began to write the book he would eventually name *Adventures of Huckleberry Finn.*

Cather's personal endeavor was distinctly artistic, and she had committed herself to the high calling of art at least twenty years before she achieved in *O Pioneers!* the sort of satisfaction that allowed her to say that she had hit the "home pasture" at last. Twain's literary development was more haphazard. He once remarked that his life consisted of a series of apprenticeships and that he was

---

1. "Preface" to *Alexander's Bridge* (New York: Alfred A. Knopf, 1922), vi, ix.

surprised to discover, at the age of thirty-seven, that he had become a "literary person." Only four years after this revelation he embarked on the writing of "Huck Finn's Autobiography" (as he had described it in a letter to W. D. Howells),[2] the book that has secured for him the reputation as something significantly more than a mere "literary person." And part of the mystery of *Huckleberry Finn* is how Twain's achievement in this book outran his qualifications to write it. But Twain too was guided by some "thing" within him, though he seems often to have lost his way. At times, in fact, he wanted to abandon the journey altogether. But he did not, and the result was a book that transmuted fact and experience into memorable fiction.

"No more beautiful or instructive example of the artist's dilemma, of the source of his passions, and how, if ever, he must lovingly resolve them, is available to us than this passion of Mark Twain, resolved in *Huckleberry Finn*." So wrote another midwestern novelist, Wright Morris. Artistic development and maturity, Morris insisted, demand more than the acquisition of literary technique; they require, as well, the recognition of the contingency of fact and the permanence of fiction. The edges of fact and fiction sometimes blurred for Twain, but in *Huckleberry Finn*, "in one moment of vision, a state of hallowed reminiscence, he seemed to grasp the distinction," and "his genius flowed into it."[3] What we know of the composition of *Huckleberry Finn* suggests not a single moment of vision, however, but several. Nevertheless, a general statement about the relation of fact to fiction Morris once made in an essay has an appropriateness to Mark Twain's relation to his book:

> We are, indeed, cunning and inscrutable creatures, mad for facts that we must turn into fiction to possess. If it's about man, it's about fiction, and the better the fiction, the more it's about. The worse the fiction, the less we have of the facts of life. If we are to be more rather than less human—one of our many stimulating options—we will turn from what we see around us, and attend to

2. *Mark Twain–Howells Letters: The Correspondence of Samuel L. Clemens and William D. Howells, 1872–1890,* 2 vols., ed. Henry Nash Smith and William M. Gibson, (Cambridge: Harvard University Press, 1960), 1:144.

3. *The Territory Ahead* (Lincoln: University of Nebraska Press, 1978), 88, 84.

the promptings within us. The imagination made us human, but *being* human, becoming more human, is a greater burden than we imagined. We have no choice but to imagine ourselves more human than we are.[4]

The facts of the composition of *Huckleberry Finn* tell us something about the fiction that is the novel. And one of the things they tell us is that Mark Twain, mainly through his identification with Huck, imagined himself more completely human than he probably was himself, and in doing so provided his readers with the same opportunity.

II

In a sense we know both too much and too little about the making of *Huckleberry Finn*. The extant evidence for its composition is of several sorts. The single most important piece of evidence is a holograph manuscript now housed in the Buffalo Public Library. This manuscript represents approximately three-fifths of the novel and consists of most of chapter 12, all of chapters 13 and 14, and chapters 22 through the concluding chapter 43, all written in Twain's beautifully clear hand. And there is the familiar "raft chapter" extracted from the novel and included in *Life on the Mississippi* (1883) and now, in the California-Iowa edition of the novel, restored to chapter 16. There are as well letters and other sorts of testimony related to *Huckleberry Finn,* and there are various references to the book in Twain's notebooks. Finally, there are the working notes for the novel, which Bernard DeVoto divided into three distinct groups (A, B, and C) and which are particularly significant in reconstructing the composition of the novel. These notes record ideas for future episodes, reminders about what Twain had already written, and notations about the vernacular speech of his characters. We know as well that

4. "If Fiction Is So Smart, Why Are We So Stupid?" in *About Fiction: Reverent Reflections on the Nature of Fiction with Irreverent Observations on Writers, Readers, and Other Abuses* (New York: Harper and Row, 1975), 182.

at least one typescript of the novel was made in two stages and that this served as the printer's copy for the first edition. Howells had the first two-fifths retyped because it was so cluttered with revisions, including some of Howells's own markings. The holograph of that portion of the manuscript of the novel was probably destroyed after that typescript was completed, and no portion of the typescript itself has survived.

On the basis of most of this evidence (not all of it was available to him), DeVoto speculated that *Huckleberry Finn* was composed in two distinct stages.[5] Chapters 1 through 16 (minus the interpolated *Walter Scott* episode and the "King Sollermun" debate) were written in the summer of 1876, for Twain wrote Howells on August 9 that he had written about four hundred manuscript pages in a month and was only partly satisfied by the result and had decided to pigeonhole or burn the novel when it was complete. The remainder, claimed De-Voto, was written in an eruptive burst of inspiration in 1883. We do know, at any rate, that on September 1, 1883, Twain wrote his English publisher that he had just finished the book.

DeVoto's account of the composition of *Huckleberry Finn* was based upon a conscientious inspection of available evidence, and it placed special emphasis on the effect that Twain's Mississippi River trip in 1882 had in revitalizing the author's interest in the "pigeonholed" manuscript of Huck's adventures. Twain made this trip to gather firsthand reacquaintance with life along the river in order to complete *Life on the Mississippi,* a book that had its origin in the simple reminiscence he published as "Old Times on the Mississippi" in 1875. For DeVoto and others, the real beneficiary of this trip was not his river book, however, but *Huckleberry Finn.* Though DeVoto had divided the working notes into three distinct groups, he assumed that all of these notes for continuing the Huck manuscript were written after that trip and offered evidence that Twain had at last discovered the "true purpose" of the book he had abandoned six years earlier. In the remaining chapters Twain would "exhibit the rich variety of life

---

5. See "Noon and the Dark," in *Mark Twain at Work* (Cambridge: Harvard University Press, 1942), 45–82.

in the great central valley," a variety that included in its diverse effects the chicanery and venality of the king and the duke, the senseless cruelty of the Bricksville loafers, and the stupid and violent attachment to clannish pride of the feuding Grangerfords and Shepherdsons.⁶ Such was the prevailing view of the making of *Huckleberry Finn* through most of the 1940s and 1950s, until Walter Blair challenged that view in 1958 with his essay "When Was *Huckleberry Finn* Written?"⁷

The working notes for *Huckleberry Finn* were written in a variety of ink colors and on different kinds of paper. Taking his cue from DeVoto that a study of the kinds of paper and ink Twain used between 1876 and 1884 might yield useful information about the dates of composition of these notes, Blair undertook an exhaustive

---

6. Ibid., 69.

7. The present essay, as any essay having to do with the composition of *Huckleberry Finn* must be, is deeply indebted to the work of Walter Blair. The indebtedness here is extensive enough to omit elaborate documentation; unless otherwise indicated, discussion of the physical evidence of composition, the state of the author's mind at the time of writing, and the several influences on the book derive in some measure from Blair's "When Was *Huckleberry Finn* Written?" (*American Literature* 30 [March 1958]: 1–25) or *Mark Twain and Huck Finn* (Berkeley and Los Angeles: University of California Press, 1960). A more recent and succinct accounting of the composition is Blair's introduction to the California-Iowa edition of *Adventures of Huckleberry Finn*.

From the substantial body of scholarship and criticism related in some way to the composition of *Huckleberry Finn,* the following might be profitably consulted as well: Louis J. Budd, "Introduction" to the facsimile edition of the manuscript of *Adventures of Huckleberry Finn* (Detroit: Gale Research, 1983), 1:ix–xx; Allison Ensor, "The Contributions of Charles Webster and Albert Bigelow Paine to *Huckleberry Finn*," *American Literature* 40 (May 1968): 222–27; Sydney Krause, "Twain's Method and Theory of Composition," *Modern Philology* 56 (February 1959): 167–77; Thomas Pauly, "Directed Readings: The Contents Tables in *Huckleberry Finn*," *Proof* 3 (1973): 63–68; and Henry Nash Smith, *Mark Twain: The Development of a Writer* (New York: Atheneum, 1967), 113–37. More recently Victor Fischer has determined, on the basis of evidence too intricate and complicated to go into here, that the composition of the feud chapters and the chapters that introduce the king and duke may have not occurred in distinct phases, for it appears that Twain was working on the Huck manuscript intermittently throughout the period between 1879 and 1883. Fischer has not yet published his findings, however, and it would be unfitting to anticipate the conclusions he may draw from his research.

and impressive investigation of Twain's writing materials during that period. He surveyed more than four hundred of Twain's letters, twenty-six of his manuscripts, and all the notebook entries he made during these years. He found that Twain used pencils, typewriters, and at least five kinds of ink; he noted the many kinds and sizes of paper that the author used in letters, notes, and manuscripts. This massive array of evidence of Twain's writing habits is dizzying in its variety and complexity—sometimes Twain used two kinds of paper in a single letter, and a manuscript of any length might contain a half a dozen kinds. But Blair was nevertheless able to discern a pattern in the evidence that he collected, one that enabled him to date the working notes and, in turn, to plot the development of the novel over those seven years.

The violet ink used in Group A of the working notes was particularly significant because Blair discovered that with only a few exceptions Twain used this color of ink sporadically between 1876 and 1880 and only when he was at Hartford, and more importantly that he ceased to use it altogether after the fall of 1880. Blair's conclusion, of course, was that these notes were written before the summer of 1880 and, therefore, that DeVoto was wrong in claiming they were written when Twain was "fresh" from his river trip in 1882.[8]

A more precise dating of Twain's working notes enabled Blair to reconsider other available evidence (including the internal evidence provided by the notes themselves) in a new light and to offer the

---

8. The complete working notes are published in DeVoto, *Mark Twain at Work*, 63–78 passim, and in Blair and Fischer's California-Iowa edition of *Huckleberry Finn*, 711–61. Blair made still other refinements on DeVoto's interpretation of the working notes. Group B of the notes consists of only two manuscript pages. Blair concluded, on the basis of the kind of paper used, that page B–1 also belongs to the period when Twain wrote Group A. Page B–2 was written separately and probably belongs to a series of notations the author made while he was going through the portion of the manuscript written in 1876, for the notes include references to page numbers in the now lost manuscript. Hence page B–2 probably also belongs to the period when Twain wrote Group A. Blair agreed with DeVoto that Group C was likely written in the summer of 1883. This last group includes reminders about what Twain had already written and suggestions for possible narrative development, only a few of which are realized in the novel.

convincing hypothesis that *Huckleberry Finn* was written in at least four rather than two stages. The first stage occurred in the summer of 1876. At that time Twain wrote the first sixteen chapters (excluding the *Walter Scott* and King Solomon episodes), or up to that point in chapter 16 where the steamboat smashes through the raft. Then, sometime in 1879–1880, he resumed the manuscript. Huck had survived the smashup and had climbed ashore to be a witness to the stupidity and needless violence of the Shepherdson-Grangerford feud. Evidently he paused halfway through this episode to write the first set of working notes for the continuation of Huck's adventures, for one of the notes indicates a belated decision to resurrect the raft and to continue the river voyage of Huck and Jim: "Back a little, CHANGE—raft only *crippled* by steamer."⁹

At some period or periods between 1880 and June 1883, Twain wrote chapters 19 and 20 and most of 21, the chapters that introduce the king and the duke and dramatize their various con games. Later, probably in March 1883, he wrote the Hamlet soliloquy and inserted it into the already completed chapter 21. At some time after that, Twain wrote the Group C notes. The following summer he completed the novel in a final explosive burst of creative inspiration or, perhaps, of simple determination to finish a book that had begun so long before. In any event Twain was so productive that he confessed to Howells in a letter dated August 22, 1883, that he himself could not believe how much he had written in so short a time.¹⁰ Blair speculates that Twain wrote two Bricksville chapters, the Wilks chapters, and the *Walter Scott* episode (part of chapter 12 and all of chapter 13) before he carried his narrative to its conclusion. Apparently the King Solomon debate was written separately (the manuscript shows that he numbered those pages 1–17 and then renumbered them to conform with the pagination of the manuscript).¹¹ It seems likely that this debate represents Twain's final contribution to the novel that had begun seven years earlier.

9. DeVoto, *Mark Twain at Work*, 67.

10. *Twain–Howells Letters* 1:438.

11. I have given a conjectural account of the significance of this episode in "'Learning a Nigger to Argue': Quitting *Huckleberry Finn*" below.

Blair's account of when *Huckleberry Finn* was written is so thoroughgoing and his conclusions so meticulously intelligent that for thirty years it has withstood the minute scrutiny of scholars and critics (including those involved in the Mark Twain Project specifically engaged in accumulating new evidence about the book). His conclusions about the stages of composition have remained pretty much intact and unchallenged. Still, charting the stages of composition of the book was but preliminary to determining its genesis as an imaginative creation. Having plotted in its essential outlines the genetic history of *Adventures of Huckleberry Finn,* Blair made it possible to give a fuller and more comprehensible story of the making of this American classic. If some of the customary beliefs about the book had to be abandoned, other hypotheses about the novel and its author might be plausibly asserted. Moreover, *Huckleberry Finn* could be more accurately placed within the full range of Twain's interests and activities during the seven-year period of its growth.

Mark Twain was a man of many enthusiasms and as many angers. He was a man so easily diverted, so constantly and busily employed in so many projects, that one is reminded of an acrobat who spins a dozen plates atop as many sticks—rushing back and forth between and among the plates to keep them spinning while starting yet another that will further scatter his attention. Blair's scholarly adventures in tracing the chronology of *Huckleberry Finn* led him to trace as well the several forces that shaped it. This he did in his "biography of a book," *Mark Twain and Huck Finn* (1960). It was a study every bit as complex and as instructive, though in a different way, as sifting through the evidence of composition, but it gave a human and circumstantial coherence to the process he had identified mostly on the basis of physical evidence.

It would be pointless to give a comprehensive survey of Blair's findings in *Mark Twain and Huck Finn.* He offers there a detailed account of Twain's activities between 1874 and 1884—an account of his reading and writings, his business affairs, his political attitudes, and his family situation. Blair chose to give greater emphasis to Twain's immediate circumstance than to the remembered experiences of his childhood in Hannibal or his pilot years on the Mississippi, because he considered the ways the author modified youthful recollection and reminiscence according to his present state of mind more important in determining how such a book came to be.

One of the conclusions Blair had drawn in "When Was *Huckleberry Finn* Written?" after determining that the first group of the working notes was written before Twain's river trip in 1882 was that Twain did not need to revisit the places of his youth in order to revitalize his imagination. He was capable in this book, as he had been in other of his writings, of "generating within himself, without external stimuli, the power to summon to his memories vivid recollections of times past and to give them form and meaning."[12] A consideration of Twain's immediate situation and state of mind disclosed as well that such vivid remembrance was spurred by his immediate present, for which the fiction served as satisfactory expression, compensation, or resolution.

III

Mark Twain and Huck Finn makes concretely and amply clear what Bernard DeVoto had also noted—namely, that *Huckleberry Finn* had its origins and peculiar motivation in a certain sort of romantic escapism. The world was too much with Twain in the early to mid-1870s. He had tried, since his marriage in 1870, to accommodate what he took to be Livy's desires for his reform but had eventually rebelled. If he had taken up wickedness again, he did so with the overly tender conscience of a backslider; and he now pretty much confined his smoking to his study and kept his cussing out of earshot. He consumed his three old-fashioneds a day with a punctuality that might support his claim that they were good for his digestion. Twain had, like Huck in *Tom Sawyer,* decided "to smoke private and cuss private, and crowd through or bust."[13]

12. Blair, "When Was *Huckleberry Finn* Written?" 24.
13. *The Adventures of Tom Sawyer, Tom Sawyer Abroad, and Tom Sawyer, Detective,*

But other things were troubling him as well. His family and friends
had been plagued by illness or death, and financial worries made his
recently completed Hartford mansion seem as much an excess as a
comfort. It was at any rate not a citadel, for the Clemenses had
constant visitors, some of them invited, and Twain was bothered by
the burden of his enormous correspondence. He was overworked by
his diversions and diverted from his work in a way that made his
literary output seem depleted or inconsequential. Added to this was
the fact that he had turned forty in November 1875. His friend John
Hay had told him that forty was the "zenith" of a man's life, the
time when one was on the "top of the hill," but Twain may have felt
he was already over it.[14] He was at least weary and pestered and
frustrated, and it was in this state of mind that he allowed himself to
dwell on Huck Finn's autobiography.

Twain had resisted Howells's urgings that he carry Tom Sawyer's
story into his adulthood, and he observed in a letter on July 5, 1875,
that such a book would have to be autobiographical. But he promised
that by and by he would "take a boy of twelve & run him on through
life (in the first person)."[15] This impulse may have combined with
another he had indulged in a final, probably discarded chapter of *Tom
Sawyer*, which recorded in some detail Huck's miserable and cramped
life at the Widow Douglas's. The opening chapter of *Huckleberry Finn*
may in fact be a rewritten version of that discarded chapter from
Huck's point of view, and even as he was reading proof for *Tom Sawyer*
at Quarry Farm, overlooking Elmira, in the summer of 1876, Twain
had begun to fulfill his promise to his readers at the conclusion of that
book to "take up the story of the younger ones again and see what
sort of men and women they turned out to be."[16] If this is so, he must
have realized almost immediately that he could not take Huck into his

---

vol. 6 of *The Works of Mark Twain,* foreword and notes by John Gerber, text established by Paul Baender (Berkeley and Los Angeles: University of California Press [in
cooperation with the University of Iowa], 1980), 259. All subsequent references are
to this edition.

14. Reported in Blair, *Mark Twain and Huck Finn,* 88.

15. *Twain–Howells Letters* 1:92.

16. *Tom Sawyer,* 260.

maturity. That summer he wrote some four hundred manuscript pages (by his mistaken reckoning he was halfway through the novel), and though it was crowded with incident his hero had aged only a few months. More importantly, he must have recognized at some level that he could better ease his own adult worries and youthful longings and speak his own dissatisfactions in the vernacular idiom of a boy who as yet had had no childhood of his own.

Quarry Farm provided the seclusion he needed to finish reading proof for *Tom Sawyer*. It provided as well the occasion and opportunity for Twain to contemplate Huck's character as he appeared in that book and to develop the suggestiveness he found there in his new novel. Huck resisted the widow's efforts to civilize him in ways that resembled Twain's own rebellion and that could be characterized as simple, boyish mischief. Huck had promised Tom in the earlier book that he would endure the widow's pestering and would stick with her so long as he could join in the high adventures Tom's proposed gang of robbers promised. But in the autobiographical story Huck is as disappointed by Tom's lies about magic and elephants and A-rabs as he had been by the widow's talk about Providence and prayer, and he likens Tom's boasts and deeds to Sunday school.

The appearance of Pap imposed a new and all too real set of circumstances on Huck. He manfully rebelled against his father (including going to school just to spite him), but after his abduction and subsequent confinement in Pap's cabin he found that it "was kind of lazy and jolly, laying off comfortable all day, smoking and fishing, and no books nor study" (30). However, when Pap got too handy with the hickory, and when he threatened to "stow" Huck in some distant hiding place, Huck plotted his own escape. Jackson's Island was a better retreat, but it was lonesome too, and when Twain introduced the slave Jim as a companion and the raft and the river as their home he had found an ideal image for lightening the load of frustrations that bore down upon him.

But the reintroduction of Jim committed the author to a different kind of narrative. Unlike his persona's companion the "Reverend" in "Some Rambling Notes of an Idle Excursion" (1877), or Harris in *A Tramp Abroad* (1880)—both modeled after Twain's friend, the minister Joseph Twichell—Jim resisted the role of straight man and butt for pranks. Though Jim had appeared as a comic figure in the opening chapters, the seriousness of his situation as a runaway slave forced upon his creator an immediate awareness of the complexity of his circumstance and character that only slowly dawned on Huck, and was sometimes forgotten by Twain himself.

When Huck and Tom played their tricks on the sleeping Jim in chapter 2, their joke had no grave consequences and in fact provided for a certain burlesque treatment. But Huck's prank with the dead rattlesnake in chapter 10 is potentially lethal and makes Huck sorry enough to make sure Jim does not find out that the snakebite is his fault. In chapter 15 Huck plays a second trick on him by convincing Jim that he merely dreamed that they had been separated in the fog. Again the joke backfires, for when he discloses the trick in order to have his laugh, Jim gives him a tongue-lashing that so affects Huck that he "humbles himself to a nigger."

Jim's situation provided a rationale for the two to drift along nights, idle away the time, and stay clear of people. But Jim's situation was fundamentally more serious than Huck's, and more serious, too, than Mark Twain's own desire to escape. For Jim could endure Miss Watson's rough treatment and her constant "pecking" at him; he could even endure, as we later learn, the enforced separation from his family. But the fearful prospect of being sold down the river was something he could not bear.

Twain's identification with his young hero enabled him to vent his feelings of constraint and frustration and to relieve symbolically the pressures that seemed to be hemming him in. But providing Huck with a runaway slave as companion meant that Twain was dragging along with him a portion of his own troubled conscience in a way that had social and personal implications. It forced upon Huck a sense of the "real" that the merely aggravating sham and pretense of the world at large could not, and presented him with a moral dilemma that a boy could not comprehend intellectually but might mysteriously solve emotionally. It also committed Huck to a course of action that was in absolute defiance of everything he took to be moral and correct. This he did when he cleverly deceived the slave traders in chapter 16 and was to do again more dramatically in chapter 31 when he had his crisis of conscience and decided to go to hell rather than turn Jim in.

But the introduction of Jim had other effects upon Twain's fiction as well. If it qualified and corrected the impulse toward a simple romantic escapism, Jim's various protective gestures gave to Huck an innocence and sense of belonging that a place under the widow's roof or in Tom's band of robbers could not. Jim's presence enfolded Huck in what Kenneth Burke would call a "preforensic circle"—an atmosphere of familiar attachment and mutual trust that some may prefer to call family but is at any rate happily free of the necessity to be on the lookout for double-dealing and masquerade.[17] The very qualities—canniness and deviousness—that Huck acquires in fending for himself, and that make him a precocious expert in the ways of the world, are at the same time obstacles to a recognizable childhood. Only by degrees does Huck learn how to respond to Jim's affection and care.

---

17. Burke uses the term in *Attitudes toward History* (Boston: Beacon Press, 1959), 209, and elsewhere. He discusses the same concept under the label "inner circle" in "The Relation between Literature and Science" (in *The Writer in a Changing World,* ed. Henry Hart, 158–71 [New York: Equinox Cooperative Press, 1937]). A passage in that essay is coincidentally pertinent to my later discussion of Twain's shift from an escapist writer to one who discovered he could embody more abstract thought in a work of regionalism: "The inner circle is essentially the childhood level of experience. Such a thought makes one realize the special appeal that 'regionalism' may have for the poetic mind. For regionalism tends simply to *extend* the perspective of intimacy and immediacy that one gets in childhood. In childhood one does not think by concepts. . . . The poet is happiest in handling material of this sort. In his scrupulous childhood, he evolves a structure of meanings, all highly intimate and personalized. And as he confronts 'new matter,' the abstract, impersonal, political, and economic matter of adult experience, his earlier integration is threatened. Some poets, when encountering this threat, tend to 'freeze' at the earlier intimate level. They continue perfecting their personalized perspective, simply ignoring the matter that lies outside its circle. I think that we get in uncritical forms of regionalism an aspect of this tendency. Whatever abstractness in the outer critical-conceptual circle they cannot humanize, they reject" (166–67). The integrations of childhood and adult experience in *Huckleberry Finn* prove that Twain did not "freeze" in the creation of his book, though the same integration may have cost him a certain narrative credibility.

Twain well recognized that the idyllic existence of Huck and Jim's life on the raft was a fragile and precarious one, and if he at first indulged in a romantic escapism in fashioning his story and in establishing an image of perfect freedom, it soon became the sort of honorable romanticism and escapism Wallace Stevens identifies as the foundation of artistic creation. In "The Noble Rider and the Sound of Words," Stevens remarks that "the pressure of reality is, I think, the determining factor in the artistic character of an era and, as well, the determining factor in the artistic character of an individual. The resistance to this pressure or its evasion in the case of individuals of extraordinary imagination cancels the pressure so far as those individuals are concerned." Such evasiveness is not to be condemned, for the art that issues out of it enriches the world and sets out to express the human soul. And if this is true, Stevens asks, "how is it possible to condemn escapism?"

> The poetic process is psychologically an escapist process. The chatter about escapism is, to my way of thinking, merely common cant. My own remarks about resisting or evading the pressure of reality mean escapism, if analyzed. Escapism has a pejorative sense which it cannot be supposed that I include in the sense in which I use the word. The pejorative sense applies where the poet is not attached to reality, where the imagination does not adhere to reality, which, for my part, I regard as fundamental.[18]

Twain's attachment to reality—not only the reality of his own immediate circumstance and the remembered evocations of his youth, but of the possibilities of his created characters and the cultural and political realities of life in the Mississippi valley "forty or fifty years ago"—and his attendant resistance to the pressures of that same reality invested his fiction with a form that transcended the narrowly personal and provincial character that impelled it. The humor at the very center of the book and the laughter it provokes, as James

18. "The Noble Rider and the Sound of Words," in Stevens's *The Necessary Angel: Essays on Reality and Imagination* (New York: Vintage Books, 1951), 22–23, 30–31.

M. Cox has observed, is itself a "relief from responsibility,"[19] but it is also Twain's artistic manner and his own peculiar form of resistance to the pressures of reality. It was not flight from fact, but a resistance to, even an evasion of the pressure of fact that prompted Twain's fiction, and this quality makes Morris's observation about the "beautiful example" of the writer's dilemma as it was eventually resolved in *Huckleberry Finn* especially acute. For Huck stands as a palpable fiction whose very existence is determined by the dogged recalcitrance of the world as it is. Or, as Roy Harvey Pearce once noted, Huck forever exists "not as an actuality but as a possibility" in a way that led Pearce to define him as the ideal type expressed in the phrase of Wallace Stevens, an "impossible possible philosopher's man."[20]

It is not likely that Twain's involvement in *Huckleberry Finn* occurred to him in anything like these terms. But his attachment to the reality of the world Huck lived and breathed in, a world Twain knew from his own experience, forced upon him in chapter 16 a decision about the narrative direction his book would take. Twain's personal experience superbly outfitted him to recall in vivid detail life along the Mississippi, all the way to New Orleans if necessary. It constituted a reservoir of memory that might be given fictional form. But his familiarity with the Ohio River (Jim's road to freedom) was insufficient to sustain his story. At any rate he let his heroes slip past Cairo in the fog and was now presented with the narrative difficulty of taking a runaway slave ever deeper into the South. In evident frustration with this dilemma Twain had a steamboat run over the raft, and it was at that point that he pigeonholed the manuscript.

Huck and Jim attributed their misfortune in missing the Ohio to the evil effect of the rattlesnake skin. And in a paragraph just previous to the smashup Huck addresses the reader on this point: "Anybody that don't believe yet, that it's foolishness to handle a snakeskin, after all that that snake-skin done for us, will believe it now, if

19. *Mark Twain: The Fate of Humor* (Princeton: Princeton University Press, 1966), 44.

20. "Yours Truly, Huck Finn," in *One Hundred Years of "Huckleberry Finn": The Boy, His Book, and American Culture; Centennial Essays,* ed. Robert Sattelmeyer and J. Donald Crowley (Columbia: University of Missouri Press, 1985), 323.

they read on and see what more it done for us" (130). This paragraph was probably inserted at some stage of revision, because had Twain envisioned Huck and Jim's future mishaps he would not have broken off his story at this point. The paragraph also allays any fears the reader might have that Jim might have died in the accident, for no further mention of Jim is made until Huck is reunited with him in the middle of chapter 18. But wrecking the raft was a gesture symbolic of Twain's own frustration with the way his story was developing, and it is by no means clear that he intended at this time to resurrect either the raft or Jim. Certainly the easiest way out of his dilemma was to get rid of Jim altogether. He could drown him or let him find his freedom or otherwise dispose of a character that was an encumbrance to Huck and his creator alike. Huck could have acquired a new companion and continued his drift downstream in a way that would have allowed Twain, through Huck, to survey southern manners and customs with greater latitude and freedom. These were some of Twain's options, but he did not choose to exercise them.

As Henry Nash Smith observes, Twain was constantly discovering meanings in his narrative as he went along and inventing the technical methods to explore them. The gestation of *Huckleberry Finn* reveals a "dialectical interplay" in Twain, a process in which "the reach of his imagination imposed a constant strain on his technical resources, and innovations of method in turn opened up new vistas before his imagination."[21] He did not, in any event, follow the path of least resistance in developing his story, and the paradoxical situation of having a runaway slave escape into the Deep South stretched his imagination to the end of its tether. Or, as Twain himself would have said, his "tank" had run dry by the end of that summer, and it would be another three years before it had sufficiently filled for him to take up his story once again.

21. *Development of a Writer,* 113.

IV

When Twain did return to Huck's autobiography, sometime in 1879–1880, a new set of circumstances defined his state of mind, and evidently he began the boy's new adventures with little thought about reviving the romantic image of a pair of lazy drifters on the Mississippi. When Huck "clum" ashore after the accident on the river, he did not pause to ponder Jim's fate or to grieve his possible death. Apparently Twain was anxious to involve Huck in the new dramatic conflicts that had inspired him to return to the novel, and it was not until he was well into the feud chapters that he stopped to record his first set of working notes and there decided that the raft should only be damaged, not destroyed. In short, Twain had other things on his mind, and he resurrected Huck to give voice to his own mature convictions.

Some three years intervened between the time Twain dropped the *Huckleberry Finn* manuscript and the time he picked it up again. During those years he had toured Germany, France, and Italy and had published an imaginative autobiographical account of his travels as *A Tramp Abroad;* and by 1880 he had written a good deal of the novel he would call *The Prince and the Pauper* (1882). In both books he was working out powerful, antagonistic feelings about elitist culture and aristocratic pretense.

Early in 1879 he wrote Howells that he wished he could give the "sharp satires on European life" his friend had mentioned, but he was in no mood for satire: "A man can't write successful satire except he be in a calm, judicial good-humor; whereas I *hate* travel, & I *hate* hotels, & I *hate* the opera, & I *hate* the Old Masters—in truth I don't ever seem to be in a good enough humor with ANYthing to *satirize* it; no, I want to stand up before it & *curse* it, and foam at the mouth."[22] Nevertheless he employed in *A Tramp Abroad* a satirical device adequate to his anger and sufficiently muted to preserve his humor. By adopting a persona who was rather more apt to question his own feelings of astonishment or revulsion when confronted by

22. *Twain–Howells Letters* 1:248–49.

senseless or violent European customs (as, for example, the student duels in Germany) than to express his contempt for the customs themselves, Twain developed a satirical strategy that he would use in the feud chapters of *Huckleberry Finn*. And in *The Prince and the Pauper* he found that he could satisfy his immediate impulse toward strong satire without risking adverse reaction by making his subject historically remote. As early as 1872 Twain had wanted to write a satire of English institutions, but his subsequent travels to England had softened him toward the British. His reading in English history reawakened his anger, however, and the result was a book that expressed his deepest dissatisfactions and at the same time could be advertised as "A Tale for Young People of All Ages."

Both of these fictional strategies entered into *Huckleberry Finn* when he began the Shepherdson-Grangerford chapters. Twain's sardonic response toward the verse of the "Sweet Singer of Michigan," Julia A. Moore, found an outlet in Huck's undoubting admiration for Emmeline Grangerford's poetic gifts. The same is true of Huck's description of the Grangerford house itself (which may have been written as early as 1876). And Twain's own mordantly satirical purposes were only thinly disguised by Huck's uncomprehending curiosity about the origin and nature of the feud itself. Huck's naïveté adequately conveyed the author's solid contempt for such timid and senseless attachment to prejudice. In Huck's eyes the tribes of Shepherdson and Grangerford are a "handsome lot of quality" (144) whose possessions and sentiments alike participate in an order of cultivation and gentility quite beyond his understanding. In Twain's, they both epitomize the sham and pretense that Twain (now an ardent Republican) had come to localize in the South and yet represent, more generally, an American version of the aristocracy that, through his recent reading about the French Revolution, Twain had come to despise to the extent that he might be described (as he in fact did describe himself a few years later) as a "Sansculotte."[23]

As Michael Davitt Bell has observed, Huck Finn exists as both a literary character and a literary device, and to collapse this distinction

---

23. Ibid., 2:595.

often results in unnecessary critical confusions because the same character is often made to serve different artistic purposes.[24] Throughout most of the feud chapters Twain used Huck as a satirical device designed to establish his own strong feelings through his narrator's naive reactions. But when Huck, in clipped and defensive understatement, reported on his reaction to Buck Grangerford's killing, Twain was dramatizing the traumatic effects of violence on his created character.

By the end of chapter 18, however, he had reinstalled Huck and Jim on the raft, where things were once again "free and easy and comfortable." He opened the next chapter with his lyrical description of how they put in the time on the river. These evocations of idyllic drift, as Walter Blair points out, could have been written at almost any time during the period from 1880 to 1883. For whenever he was vexed by the pressures of reality, Twain allowed his imagination to dwell on the possibilities of escape and seclusion. But during most of the second phase of composition he had been more aggressively ironic in his treatment of the bugbears of his imagination: aristocratic values, cloying sentimentality, and unnecessary violence.

This sort of control over his material signals a shift in Twain's creative process as it developed alongside the accumulating pages of the manuscript. In the first phase of composition he had found the means to project his own complex feelings of frustration into his created character in a way that required only the simplest explanation of their causes. A whippoorwill's song might convey his loneliness, and a stiff collar or the widow's "pecking," his feelings of repression. But when he returned to the manuscript Twain had bigger fish to fry, and the result was that, though he still identified with him, he absorbed Huck into himself rather than the other way round. He made his young vernacular hero serve the mature purposes of his creator. In a word, Twain's manner and motivation had progressed from those of an escapist writer to those of a professionally skillful

24. See Bell, "Mark Twain, 'Realism,' and *Huckleberry Finn*," in *New Essays on "Huckleberry Finn,"* ed. Louis J. Budd (Cambridge: Cambridge University Press, 1985), 50.

one, one whose imaginative impulses were the same but whose technical means were more rational and whose artistic effects were more calculated.

This same imaginative process obtained when he wrote the king and duke chapters, though the motivating circumstances had changed. In 1881 Twain hired his nephew, Charles Webster, as his business agent. Webster tackled the job with a dramatic energy and aggressiveness that may have inclined him to invent tasks (and get results) over and above the regular duties of a financial manager. But there was no doubt that Twain needed such a manager, for his finances were always complicated and his extravagant expenditures and investments in the early 1880s bordered on caprice. Twain's financial worries were legitimate enough, but Webster added to his uncle's anxiousness by convincing him that he was being cheated right and left by scoundrels and con men. Webster had a questionable knack for discovering cheats, and Twain, constitutionally suspicious anyway, was easily persuaded that he was being defrauded. Something of this suspiciousness went into the creation of his famous rascals, the king and the duke, whose diverse talents as confidence men adequately symbolized the various cheats, from plumbers to publishers, that Twain was convinced were attempting to hoodwink him. And by having these characters adopt titles of royalty Twain could continue his burlesque of aristocratic values.

The king and duke are composite figures, partly inspired by Twain's "recollection vaults" (178) and partly by present acquaintance. As he had done in the feud chapters, in fashioning his homespun picaros he also drew upon the reading in southwestern humorists he was doing for the volume that would eventually appear as *Mark Twain's Library of Humor* (1888). The king and duke were so characterized by humbug, chicanery, and pretense that they became objects of contempt and figures of fun. But as fictional devices this pair provided their creator with a double opportunity. He could satirize *in them* such despicable or laughable qualities as false eloquence, venality, backbiting, deception, or invented claims to privilege; and he could satirize *through them* the ignorant, credulous, or sentimental victims who were their prey.

Twain's rogues also solved a narrative problem for the author: for they enabled him to continue to move Huck and Jim further downstream. They effectively commandeered the raft and, by printing up a reward poster for Jim, devised a way to travel daytime and make temporary excursions onshore to ply their trade. This, in turn, provided Huck with the opportunity to describe loathsome backwater behavior and to witness the Boggs shooting. By 1880 Twain had begun to develop a general bitterness that he would succinctly express as a larger contempt for the "damned human race," and by freeing Huck to wander about town and observe the manners and customs of a representative cross section of humanity Twain's scorn could be delivered broadcast.

V

In his rendering of the Bricksville loafers and the Boggs shooting in chapter 21 Twain had already begun to dramatize his disdain of the common man and woman. When he settled down in Elmira in June 1883 to finish his book, he began with Colonel Sherburn's verbal attack on the mob. Twain had prepared his readers for a lynching and had several times in his working notes made references to such a scene. But he had also conveyed more subtly in chapter 21 his distrust of the mob, and by the time he came to write chapter 22, his contempt for the crowd outstripped his contempt for the southern aristocrat.[25] Colonel Sherburn, who had lived in the North and had been raised in the South, spoke the author's own convictions about the cowardice of the "average" man in a way that made him as much a hero in chapter 22 as he had been a villain in chapter 21.

Life on the Mississippi and *Huckleberry Finn* had a cross-pollinating effect upon one another. The Huck manuscript provided germs for

25. For a discussion of the significance of the crowd in *Huckleberry Finn* see Nicolas Mills, *The Crowd in American Literature* (Baton Rouge: Louisiana State University Press, 1986), 66–75.

development of certain portions of *Life on the Mississippi,* and Twain had lifted the raft episode from it and put it in chapter 3 of his "standard" work on the Mississippi. In turn, Twain's return to the river in 1882 and his writing about the modern South had stimulated certain youthful memories that might pay dividends in *Huckleberry Finn.* But nostalgia had combined with outrage, and Twain had excised from *Life on the Mississippi* two chapters of strident social criticism and had generally toned down his more virulent attacks upon the South. The intensity of his antisouthern feeling remained, however, and in fact may have been exacerbated by this same restraint. In any event the author allowed Sherburn, rather than Huck, to speak his contempt in the scene that began the last phase of composition of the novel.

Twain soon resumes Huck's persona, however, and his methods of satire become more familiar. He concluded the chapter with Huck at the circus, where he worries over the drunken bareback rider. The comedy of this episode was meant to comment upon the seriousness of the Boggs episode in the previous chapter and is one of the more conspicuous examples of satirical pairings of incidents that occur throughout the book. But the development of the circus scene as a counterstatement to the Boggs episode points to the workmanlike attitude Twain brought to his book that summer.

By 1883 *Adventures of Huckleberry Finn* had become a commercial venture, and it is difficult to tell whether inspiration or simple determination supplied the kind of motivation that allowed Twain to produce so many pages of manuscript so quickly and, by his own account, so effortlessly.[26] He had been disappointed by the sales of *The Prince and the Pauper* and *Life on the Mississippi* and, soon after he finished *Huckleberry Finn,* decided to publish the book himself under the imprint of Chas. L. Webster & Co. The last phase of composition betrays something of the practical attitude of a professional novelist intent on finishing a book in which he had invested considerable

26. In August 1883 Twain wrote Howells how delicious his productivity was, confessing that "nothing is half so good as literature hooked on a Sunday on the sly" (*Twain–Howells Letters* 1:438).

time and energy. At any rate Twain pushed toward his conclusion and most days found the going easy.

In the last half of *Huckleberry Finn* the author was able to make the most of his invention. He had recorded in his working notes a few episodes he wanted to develop (the circus rider incident and the obscene Royal Nonesuch were included, but fortunately Twain's desire to have Huck and Jim and Tom explore the countryside on an elephant remained unfulfilled), and he had made elaborate notes for the evasion scene. But this second half is remarkable for its relative lack of incident. The improvisations of the Wilks funeral and the evasion at least are stretched to the point of artificiality and seem to have less to do with resolving the inner tensions of the author than with delivering broad and popular comedy. These episodes had been prepared for in advance, and the notes show that the evasion had been planned with a good deal of calculation. But the notes also show that Twain carefully reread the portion of the manuscript that he had already completed, and the most interesting and memorable events are those that drew upon the emotional attitudes he had established in the earlier portions and now contemplated and probed for their implications.

The proletarian sympathies Twain had acquired a few years before persisted, despite his distrust of the mob, and they became localized and found a certain focus in his attitude toward Jim. Twain's last group of working notes reveals an interest in developing Jim's character more fully. He twice reminded himself that Jim has a wife and two children and anticipated the moment in chapter 23 where Jim grieves because he believes he will never see his family again and, in turn, recalls his unintended cruelty to his infant daughter, whom he discovered to be deaf and dumb. Jim's mourning makes Huck believe that Jim "cared just as much for his people as white folks does for theirn. It don't seem natural, but I reckon it's so" (201). This incident immediately follows, and therefore comments on, Huck's description of the conduct of "Henry the Eight," who used to marry a new wife every day and "chop her head off" the next morning. And it comments as well on the feigned deaf and dumbness of the king in the next chapter.

Twain also wrote in his working notes: "Back yonder, Huck reads & tells about monarchies & kings &c. So Jim stares when he learns the rank of these 2."[27] Again, Twain was preparing to use Jim's reaction rather than Huck's as the vehicle for his satire, and the "back yonder" became the interpolated chapter 14, where Huck describes the "style" kings and dukes put on. The only king Jim is familiar with is King Solomon, whom he knows "by de back" (95). Solomon's apparent insensitivity regarding the child he was going to chop in two derives, so Jim believes, from the way he was "raised" and his circumstance. A man, such as Jim, "dat's got on'y one er two chillen" cannot afford to be wasteful of them, but Solomon, who has some "five million," may treat them as expendable items of property.

This debate apparently satisfied the author's intention rather telegraphically recorded in another note—"Solomon with child by de hine laig."[28] And Huck and Jim's debate about why a Frenchman "doan' . . . *talk* like a man" (which concludes the chapter) probably derived from a stray remark Twain had written at the end of chapter 20: "I found Jim had been trying to get [the king] to talk French, so he could hear what it was like" (176).

Chapter 14 was written separately, and probably after Twain had taken his story through "Chapter the Last." In any event it not only prepares the reader for Jim's reaction to the king and duke but gives to a slave a native intelligence, a righteous indignation, and a vernacular eloquence that had not been fully dramatized before. Moreover, Jim can get riled by the example of Solomon as a man who seemingly treats his children and wives as chattels, and who would rather live in the confusion of a "bo'd'n house" than, as Jim believes a truly wise man would, "buil' a biler-factry" (94). Jim's reaction to Solomon is the reaction of a slave to the southern mentality, which immorally prefers the chaos of a "harem" of kept servants to sensible industrialization.

If chapter 14 was written out of the felt necessity to add to the picture Twain had drawn of Jim, Huck's recollection of Jim's self-

27. DeVoto, *Mark Twain at Work,* 75.
28. Ibid.

sacrifice and affection in chapter 31 offers a consolidated picture of
Jim's generosity of spirit:

> [I] got to thinking over our trip down the river; and I see Jim before
> me, all the time, in the day, and in the night-time, sometimes
> moonlight, sometimes storms, and we a floating along, talking and
> singing, and laughing. But somehow I couldn't seem to strike no
> places to harden me against him, but only the other kind. I'd see
> him standing my watch on top of his'n, stead of calling me—so I
> could go on sleeping; and see him how glad he was when I come
> back out of the fog; and when I come to him again in the swamp,
> up there where the feud was; and such-like times; and would al-
> ways call me honey, and pet me, and do everything he could think
> of for me, and how good he always was; and at last I struck the
> time I saved him by telling the men we had small-pox aboard, and
> he was so grateful, and said I was the best friend old Jim ever had
> in the world, and the *only* one he's got now. (269–70)

It is this catalog of recollections that decides Huck on going to hell
rather than turning Jim in. One can easily imagine that (as he studied
the completed portion of the manuscript, and as the working notes
to some extent reveal) Twain similarly recollected the accumulated
examples of Jim's humanity and generosity of spirit and discovered
in him a fit emblem for the best there is in the common lot, one for
whom one might even risk everlasting fire. In this sense Jim plays a
role analogous to the peasant Gerasim in Tolstoy's *The Death of Ivan
Ilyich*—a figure of such warm and authentic sympathies that in the
midst of misery and doubt he inspires a mystical faith in human
possibility and, by his example, urges a revaluation of conventional
political pieties.

In the tangle of contrived narrative improbabilities Huck's decision
to go to hell stands out as the most improbable event of all. For it
gathers together in a single dramatic moment the implications of the
fiction Twain was creating and runs absolutely counter to what he
believed to be the incontestable facts of the world. But unlike those
improbable details and incidents designed to prolong or resolve dramatic conflicts—such as the broken arm of William Wilks, the mystery of the tattoo, the appearance of Tom Sawyer with his ever

proliferating plans for the evasion, or the implausible guilty conscience of the widow that resulted in her freeing Jim before her
death—Huck's decision to go to hell is not mere contrivance. Rather
it is a fiction that affirms a certain faith in the possibility of human
freedom and nobility and runs counter to Twain's announced cynicism.

By the time the author settled down to finish his novel in the
summer of 1883, he had formed a set of generalized convictions and
had embraced the deterministic philosophic position he had articu-
lated a few months earlier in "What Is Happiness?"—a paper he had
delivered at the Monday Evening Club. The conclusions he drew in
this lecture, he later recalled, were straightforward and absolute:
there is no such thing as personal merit; man is merely a "machine
automatically functioning"; "no man ever does a duty for duty's
sake"; "there is no such thing as free will and no such thing as self-
sacrifice."[29] Some years before Twain had privately recorded similar
beliefs in the margins of his copy of W. E. H. Lecky's *History of
European Morals,* and his subsequent reading and experience had
only fortified those convictions. Twain's philosophic opinions had
to some extent always been present in *Huckleberry Finn,* but in this
last phase of composition they entered into the novel at some expense to narrative credibility.

In *Life on the Mississippi* Twain had recalled the emotional quality
of youth as "a time when the happenings of life were not the natural
and logical results of great general laws, but of special orders, and
were freighted with very precise and distinct purposes—partly punitive in intent, partly admonitory; and usually local in application."[30]
At odd moments Twain had abandoned this quality in the last half of
the novel and allowed Huck to speak with a latitude of experience
and moral authority beyond his years and beyond his immediate
interests. He permitted him to conclude on the cruelty of the "human race" and make comments about the "average" man or woman
(something Colonel Sherburn could do more plausibly because he
had traveled in the North and lived in the South and had acquired the

29. Quoted in Blair, *Mark Twain and Huck Finn,* 337.
30. *Life on the Mississippi* (New York: Viking Penguin, 1986), 375.

cynicism of age and experience); and he had had Huck make such observations as "kings is kings" or "Take them all around, they're a mighty ornery lot. It's the way they're raised" (200).

One could not say that Huck had become worldly wise or jaded, but his commentary sometimes tends toward general observation at the expense of local assertion. The qualities of stupefaction and surprise that he had before displayed and that served as satirical strategy are frequently shifted onto Jim, and the particularity of experience is too often reserved for the purely technical virtuosity of the humbug of the king and duke or the childish pranks of the evasion.

Everything Twain rationally thought to be true militated against Jim's recorded self-sacrifice and Huck's dramatic decision to help him to freedom. But these were fictions that mysteriously commanded belief, and they were latent in the emotional attitudes Twain had established in earlier portions of the novel. Twain himself recalled, in 1895, that Huck's first bout with his conscience in chapter 16 represented a contest between a "sound heart" and a "deformed conscience" and that "conscience suffers defeat."[31] Huck's white lie to the slave traders in that chapter suggested the more affecting decision in chapter 31, and the latter is more powerful because Huck actively chooses what he takes to be an everlasting damnation in the "bad place" Miss Watson had so vividly described to him.

The evasion chapters undoubtedly compromise the purity of Huck's purpose, but they do not entirely overthrow it. And Twain may have anticipated the erosion of Huck's moral dignity in those chapters where Tom Sawyer superintends their high jinks. In any event he seems to have written the interpolated *Walter Scott* episode just before he began the Phelps chapters. DeVoto suggested that the primary motivation for inserting this episode was to provide Huck with the history books he reads to Jim.[32] This may be so, but it would have been much simpler to have included those books with the "truck" they took off the floating house in chapter 9. Blair argues,

31. Quoted in Blair, *Mark Twain and Huck Finn,* 143.
32. *Mark Twain at Work,* 62.

more plausibly, that Twain had his eye out for opportunities to repeat "motifs with variations" and that this scene of a real robber gang provided a dramatic parallel to Tom Sawyer's gang of robbers in chapter 3.[33] Certainly the name of the steamboat evokes an image of the romanticism so characteristic of Tom. But the same episode also provides a parallel to the evasion scene, and with a significant variation.

Huck himself invites the comparison when he rebukes Jim's hesitancy to board the wreck and reminds him that Tom would never miss the chance for such an adventure. When they find that they are trapped on the *Walter Scott* with real murderers, however, Huck instantly recognizes that this is no time for "sentimentering" (86). After he and Jim escape in the gang's boat, Huck begins to worry about the men and to hatch a plot that will get them out of their scrape. His resolution and plan are acted out with efficiency and dispatch and are happily free of the romantic impulse. This scene provides a dramatic contrast to the evasion episode. Huck may call the experience an "adventure," but his natural sympathy for the other Jim (the murderer Jim Turner) and his practical attempt to rescue him and the others demonstrate Huck's native decisiveness, uncorrupted by the influence of Tom Sawyer. The evasion in its way is as "mixed-up en splendid" (340) as Jim says it is, but Twain had to some extent preserved the purity of Huck's sound heart by dramatizing his reaction to the moral emergency aboard the *Walter Scott.*

The final two chapters of *Huckleberry Finn* hastily tie up the loose ends of Twain's narrative. Jim learns that he had been set free in Miss Watson's will two months earlier. The mystery of Tom's cooperation in Jim's rescue is explained by the fact that he thought it great fun to "set a free nigger free." And Huck learns that Pap was the dead man aboard the floating house. The end of *Huckleberry Finn* is inexcusably happy—Jim owns himself, Huck is rid of Pap and free to use his six thousand dollars to sponsor a new adventure in the Indian Territory, and the bullet Tom received in the leg is now proudly worn around his neck for all the world to see. But Twain concluded on the

---

33. *Mark Twain and Huck Finn,* 347.

same note of resistance to the pressures of civilization that had been
in the book from the beginning, and by having Huck light out for the
Territory ahead of his comrades, he promised his readers and committed himself to a continuation of their adventures in another book.

For the next seven months Twain worked on several projects and
may have actually begun to write his promised sequel in *Huck Finn
and Tom Sawyer among the Indians;* at least he did some reading for it.
But much of his time was spent preparing his manuscript for publication. He made many revisions and did some rewriting, nearly
always with an artistic intent rather than out of deference to contemporary literary taste or personal squeamishness, and by mid-
April 1884 had mailed off the manuscript. He carefully supervised
E. W. Kemble's illustrations for the book and Webster's promotional
campaign to sell it by subscription, and he embarked on a lecture
tour with George Washington Cable, in part as an effort to promote
sales of the novel. He also had to put up with the aggravation of the
technical problems of supplying his book with a heliotype of a bust
of himself as a frontispiece and the obscene joke of some mischief-
maker who had defaced the plate of Kemble's illustration of Huck
standing before Aunt Sally and Uncle Silas.[34] But at last the book
was complete. It was published in England and Canada in December
1884 and in the United States the following February.

VI

The seven-year genesis of *Huckleberry Finn* eventuated in a book
that was more hopeful than its happy ending might suggest. For it
made potent, and in a thoroughly original and unstarched idiom, a
drama of human possibility that transcended its narrowly human

34. For an account of Twain's decision to include this heliotype and the possible
reasons for it see Louis J. Budd, "'A Noble Roman Aspect' of *Adventures of Huckleberry
Finn,*" in *One Hundred Years of "Huckleberry Finn": The Boy, His Book, and American
Culture; Centennial Essays,* ed. Robert Sattelmeyer and J. Donald Crowley (Columbia:
University of Missouri Press, 1985), 26–40.

origins. "Give us a new work of genius of any kind," wrote Willa Cather in an open letter in defense of "escapism" in literature, "and if it is alive, and fired with some more vital feeling than contempt, you will see how automatically the old and false makes itself air before the new and true."[35] *Huckleberry Finn* is brimming with contempt, or at least feelings of anger and frustration, but it is also alive with the feeling and the fiction of human possibility.

The novel made vivid an original image, or several images really, of nobility in tatters: the absurd image of Jim in a dress forgoing his chance for freedom in order to nurse his wounded tormentor, Tom Sawyer; of Huck sitting in a wigwam choosing between everlasting and everlasting; or of Huck and Jim together, forming what Twain once called a "community of misfortune," floating down the Mississippi River on a hot summer night.[36] And there is some evidence that Twain wanted to highlight those same qualities.

Three of Twain's most significant revisions, as Blair has pointed out, signal the final emphasis the author wanted to give to his book. He trimmed the excessively rhetorical eloquence from Colonel Sherburn's speech and made it more colloquial and therefore more local and authentic. He supplemented the scene of Jim's homesickness with the passages that disclose the man's sense of regret for the way he had treated his daughter. And he added enough to Huck's struggle with his conscience to rid the scene of any tinge of burlesque and to give it the sort of memorable emphasis it has in the printed book.

The attempt to establish such nobility on so slight and improbable a foundation as the adventures of a barely literate and necessarily suspicious boy provided Twain with (to borrow the language of Henry James) "as interesting and as beautiful a difficulty as you could wish."[37] The difficulties were unsought, however, and the solutions were sometimes improvised or finessed. And there are gaps in the narrative logic of the book big enough to throw a dog

35. "Escapism: A Letter to the *Commonweal,*" in *Willa Cather on Writing: Critical Studies on Writing as an Art* (New York: Alfred A. Knopf, 1949), 26.

36. Quoted in Blair, *Mark Twain and Huck Finn,* 143.

37. James, "Preface" to the New York edition of *Portrait of a Lady,* in *The Art of the Novel: Critical Prefaces* (New York: Charles Scribner's Sons, 1962), 51.

through. But the novel is sustained by its rendering of life rather than by a formal narrative coherence, and the manifold impulses that produced it call into question the desire of critics to find a unified intention or an artistic wholeness in works of the imagination. The enduring interest of the book derives from its quiet affirmations rather than its satire, however brilliant.

"There is no element more conspicuously absent from contemporary poetry than nobility," observed Wallace Stevens in a passage that has a special relevance to *Huckleberry Finn*:

> There is no element that poets have sought after, more curiously and more piously, certain of its obscure existence. Its voice is one of the inarticulate voices which it is their business to overhear and to record. The nobility of rhetoric is, of course, a lifeless nobility. . . . For the sensitive poet, conscious of negations, nothing is more difficult than the affirmations of nobility and yet there is nothing that he requires of himself more persistently, since in them and in their kind, alone, are to be found those sanctions that are the reasons for his being and for that occasional ecstasy, or ecstatic freedom of the mind, which is his special privilege.[38]

That Twain's cynicism and skepticism made him supremely "conscious of negations" is a familiar truth. That he experienced in the writing of his masterpiece an "occasional ecstasy, or ecstatic freedom of mind," scarcely less so. Something of that ecstasy must have derived from the satisfaction that came from finding, in the tangle of his material and the meanness he knew to be the world, the room to affirm as well as condemn. For Wallace Stevens, and one may suppose for Twain as well, the capacity to affirm nobility as a permanent fiction forever at odds with the contingency of fact has less to do with artistic freedom than it does with the power of the imagination over events. "It is the violence from within that protects us from a violence from without. It is the imagination pressing back against the pressure of reality. It seems, in the last analysis, to have some-

38. "The Noble Rider and the Sound of Words," in Stevens's *The Necessary Angel,* 35.

thing to do with our self-preservation; and that, no doubt, is why the expression of it, the sound of its words, helps us to live our lives."[39]

In the making of *Huckleberry Finn,* and virtually from the beginning, Twain had resisted the pressures of reality by the efforts of his imagination and in a voice he eventually made his own. Nothing about the book commanded Twain's more minute attention than the sounds of its words. His working notes disclose how exactingly he had overheard and recorded the otherwise inarticulate voices of his created characters, and even if we did not have Twain's "Explanatory" to tell us that the book is a vernacular tour de force, the novel itself shows how absolutely he earned the evident pride he took in its language. But the language of the novel, the angle of its vision, the ample reach of its imagining, did more than retrieve the life of the Mississippi Valley, now 150 years past. In part, the achievement of the *Adventures of Huckleberry Finn* is revealed in its creative vision, for it showed how completely Twain might imagine things as bad as they can be, and better than they are. The book provided its author, as it has its readers, with a means to resist the pressures from without. It is a novel that, finally, may have to do with something as improbable as self-preservation.

39. Ibid., 36.

LIFE IMITATING ART
Huckleberry Finn and Twain's
Autobiographical Writings

Cyril: What do you mean by saying life, "poor, probable, uninteresting human life," will try to reproduce the marvels of art? I can quite understand your objection to art being treated as a mirror. You think it would reduce genius to the position of a cracked looking glass. But you don't mean to say that you seriously believe that life imitates art, that life is in fact the mirror, and art the reality?
Vivian: Certainly, I do.

—Oscar Wilde, *Decay of Lying* (1889)

I

ON MARCH 1, 1883, Mark Twain wrote William Dean Howells and reported on a lecture he had attended the previous evening given by "an idiot by the name of Stoddard." Twain found the stereopticon pictures John L. Stoddard showed full of interest but the lecturer's comments about them "chuckleheaded" and wished Stoddard had kept "still" or had "died in the first act."[1] Nevertheless, Twain evidently approved of the lecturer's description of "how re-

1. *Mark Twain–Howells Letters: The Correspondence of Samuel L. Clemens and William D. Howells, 1872–1890,* 2 vols., ed. Henry Nash Smith and William M. Gibson (Cambridge: Harvard University Press, 1960), 1:426–29.

tired tradesmen and farmers in Holland load a lazy scow with the family and the household effects and then loaf along the waterways of the Low Country all summer long, paying no visits, receiving none, and just lazying a heavenly life out in their own unpestered society, and doing their literary work, if they have any, wholly uninterrupted." Twain obviously envied this lazy and unpestered existence and felt Howells would as well: "If you had hired such a boat and sent for us we should have a couple of satisfactory books ready for the press now with no marks of interruption, vexatious weariness, and other hellishness visible upon them anywhere." The editors of the Twain–Howells correspondence comment on this portion of the letter: "The effect upon Mark Twain of Stoddard's slides depicting a lazy existence aboard a Dutch scow suggests that he may have taken up the MS of *Huckleberry Finn* again, after driving himself hard to complete *Life on the Mississippi*." However, Twain's "recollection" of this portion of Stoddard's lecture appears to have been imaginative invention, not timely reaction.

If Stoddard's published collection of his illustrated talks contains "the identical discourses" he had delivered on tours for some eighteen years, as the subtitle to the collected lectures indicates, then he made no mention of retired farmers lazily floating on a canal in a scow. The only printed passage that resembles Twain's recollection is this:

> Many of the barges in Amsterdam form the abodes of people who have no other homes. Among a certain class of Hollanders, when a young man has saved or borrowed money enough he buys a huge, broad-shouldered boat; and like the Patriarch Noah, leads into it not only his family, but also all the animals of which he is possessed, including poultry, hogs, even cows. Thenceforth he is independent; and as the master of a floating house, stable, farmyard, and express cart, all in one, and never absent from his family, he transports loads of merchandise from town to town, and even sells a few superfluous eggs, or a little milk.[2]

It is possible, of course, that Twain was recollecting an impromptu remark, not properly a part of the written lecture, but if Stoddard

2. *John L. Stoddard's Lectures* (Boston: Balch Bros. Co., 1898), 7:193–94.

made such a remark, it went against the whole tenor of his talk, for he consistently portrayed the Dutch as an industrious, persevering, ingenious people whose only occasion for relaxation was during the winter months when they might skate or glide down the frozen canals and visit friends and relatives. More likely, however, Twain summoned this image, quite unconsciously, from his own fiction— from the not yet completed *Huckleberry Finn.*

In itself, this discrepancy between fact and fiction is relatively insignificant. But it does provoke certain interesting, if unanswerable questions. Did Twain really believe he had heard Stoddard describe retired farmers loafing along the waterways? Certainly he had no reason to lie or to fictionalize the account of his experience in a private, informal letter to a trusted friend. Had Twain drawn the inference from this image that he would have desired and profited by such an existence while completing *Life on the Mississippi,* free from interruptions and other vexations? Or was the process all the other way round? Had those actual feelings of "hellishness" prompted the familiar image of escape and drift he had created several years before, in the first phase of composing *Huckleberry Finn*? In short, was the report on the Stoddard lecture an instance of factual description or of life imitating art? Either alternative is possible, for Twain possessed a projective as well as an assimilative imagination. It is equally possible that Twain did not recognize that he was inventing rather than reporting on an event, for, as Justin Kaplan has observed, the creative unconscious lay closer to the surface in Twain than in most writers.[3] In fact, Twain described himself as the "amanuensis" of his own art, a servant to the mysterious operations of his own creative imagination. In either case, it is clear that Mark Twain was identifying with the fictional hero of *Huckleberry Finn* and preferring that outcast's imagined situation to his own. It was this sort of identification that sometimes supplied the imaginative and emotional coherence that Twain's reports on his own experiences lacked.

Ever since the publication of Walter Blair's "When Was *Huckleberry*

3. *Mr. Clemens and Mark Twain: A Biography* (New York: Simon and Schuster, 1966), 253.

Finn Written?" we have been able to examine the influences upon
the composition of that novel, and Blair himself did so exhaustively
in *Mark Twain and Huck Finn* (1960). Often we may observe in the
works written during the years when the manuscript of *Huckleberry
Finn* was "pigeonholed" tentative rehearsals for a return to that book,
anticipations of episodes and themes, unconscious percolations that,
once the author's "tank" filled, would be dramatized in his novel.
However, we know as well that Twain's imagination also worked in
"reverse" (as Blair put it), that the fiction of *Huckleberry Finn* also
spilled over into his purportedly autobiographical writing. But that
reverse operation has not been sufficiently charted, and, as Kaplan
has justly remarked, Twain's reshaping of his own biography possesses its own kind of truth.[4] To look at familiar evidence in this way
is not to add substantially to what we already know but to regard it
in a new light, and it allows us to measure, however vaguely, the
degree and nature of the author's involvement with his creation, to
implicate Twain in his book, by identifying not how much of his life
was put into it, but how much of the book was put into his life, or
rather the autobiographical representation of his life. For Twain,
Huck Finn seems to have represented not the boy he had been but
the boy he wished he had been. And, though the basis of his identification with Huck surely began in simple envy of Huck's free and
unpestered situation, that basis changed during the seven-year gestation of the novel. Huck became the hero of his own life in a way that
Twain personally admired and, in the end, fictitiously attributed to
his own history. Although the author finished *Huckleberry Finn* in the
autumn of 1883, the book was not finished with him until he published
"The Private History of a Campaign That Failed" in December 1885.

II

The first autobiographical piece Twain published after he set aside
the manuscript of *Huckleberry Finn* in late August 1876, liking it only

4. Ibid., "Preface," n.p.

"tolerably well," was a four-installment series of sketches for the *Atlantic* about his trip to Bermuda with Joseph Twichell in May 1877. "Some Rambling Notes of an Idle Excursion" is flat and uninspired, though it begins promisingly enough as an account of a trip of "pure recreation" that will provide the occasion to be absolutely "free and idle."[5] But Twain forfeited whatever narrative opportunity an aimless excursion with a companion offered in preference for the anecdotal, and the relation between himself and the "Reverend" is never adequately developed. Perhaps because Twain placed his narrative persona under no particular obligation, no dramatic conflict occurred to him. In any event, his subsequent efforts to write a book about his travels in Germany, Switzerland, and northern Italy the next year seem to have begun in the same way, for much of the anecdotal material in *A Tramp Abroad* was written before he discovered a narrative plan for the book.[6] It was not until August 1878, after Twichell joined him in Europe, that Twain hit upon the "joke" that provided a narrative foundation to unify his already completed burlesques, tales, and legends. He would appear as an authentic pedestrian, in proper costume, but, as he told Howells, "mount the first conveyance that offers, making but slight explanation or excuse, and endeavoring to seem unconscious that this is not legitimate pedestrianizing."[7]

By casting Twichell as an agent named Harris whom he could assign to do his traveling for him, Twain provided his narrative persona with a mischievousness that complemented his apparent naïveté. In effect, he was Tom Sawyer again and might delegate his felt responsibilities to another. But there was a Huck Finn quality in this narrative persona as well, for he steadily resisted the obligation to become enlightened and civilized by the European experience. Thus, Twain found narrative justification for his already written burlesques of Wagnerian opera and his own attempts to learn Ger-

5. Reprinted in vol. 19 of *The Writings of Mark Twain* (New York: Gabriel Wells, 1923), 242.

6. Hamlin Hill discusses the composition of *A Tramp Abroad* in *Mark Twain and Elisha Bliss* (Columbia: University of Missouri Press, 1964), 132–48.

7. *Twain–Howells Letters* 1:248–50.

man and permitted himself to lampoon Turner and Titian and to display his seemingly guileless pride in his own crude drawings, which he juxtaposed to those of professional illustrators. These masks must have proved an antidote to the "smileless stare of solemn admiration" Twain felt shortly after he arrived in Germany,[8] but they also permitted him a creative latitude his own proper voice was incapable of. "A man can't write successful satire except he be in a calm judicial good-humor," he wrote Howells, ". . . in truth I don't ever seem to be in a good enough humor with ANYthing to *satirize* it; no, I want to stand up before it & *curse* it, and foam at the mouth."[9]

Incapacitated by his own indignation, at times Twain found he could convey his own contempt by simply displaying an undiluted sense of admiration and stupefaction. He did this when he wrote the chapters on student duels in Germany. The description of the "knightly graces" of this bloody sport is handled in much the same way he handled the feud chapters of *Huckleberry Finn* when he wrote them in 1879–1880; he reports on the duels matter-of-factly and ironically calls into question not the custom itself but his own feelings of repulsion as somehow being an untutored reaction to venerable European tradition. And, as Huck does in describing the killing of Buck Grangerford in chapter 18 of the novel, he refuses to go into "details" about the most brutal exchanges. There is anticipation of the novel, too, in chapter 24, in which his misplaced sympathy for a meanly dressed and evidently embarrassed parishioner, whom he eventually discovers is the Empress of Germany, resembles Huck's sympathetic response to the supposed drunken bareback rider in the circus.

These instances foreshadow Twain's treatment of certain episodes in *Huckleberry Finn,* but he was recollecting what he had already written when he imaginatively "chartered" a raft for a journey down the river Neckar. This invented account of a raft trip occupies only five chapters of *A Tramp Abroad,* and much of that space is given over to local legends and other interpolated matter. Indeed, from a practical point of view, this raft is simply a "conveyance" and fits neatly

8. Ibid., 227–28.
9. Ibid., 248–50.

into the planned "joke" of the book. But there may have been more than literary convenience involved in transporting Huck's raft to Germany; it was as well a private evocation of the idyllic mood he had already created in his novel and an identification of himself with the easy circumstances of Huck Finn.

His confessed "hate" for Europe and homesickness for America may have contributed something to his motives for creating this episode, and a lazy drift on a river probably served as symbolic compensation for his personal feelings of anger and vexation. Certainly, Twain recommended such a voyage to his reader, and no doubt the image provided a salve to his immediate situation: "The motion of a raft is the needful motion; it is gentle, and gliding, and smooth, and noiseless; it calms down all feverish activities, it soothes to sleep all nervous hurry and impatience; under its restful influence all the troubles and vexations and sorrows that harass the mind vanish away, and existence becomes a dream, a charm, a deep and tranquil ecstasy."[10] Indeed, in these chapters Twain consistently draws upon the contrast between the soothing ease on the river and human sorrow and vexation on shore.

On land there is drudgery (represented by the women he observes working in the fields, or those he remembers who work in town), the busy activity of progress (symbolized by the massive and destructive construction work on a railroad that levels mountains and tunnels through bluffs), and sleepless nights (experienced by young "Z" at the Naturalist Tavern). And there is the felt constraint of propriety, which makes the narrator confused and uncomfortable (epitomized by the perplexing custom of bowing or the rules of dress for admittance to a ball or the baffling and contradictory regulations governing admission into the student corps, all described in chapter 17). On the raft, however, Twain is content; he observes naked children happily swimming and describes peaceful landscapes. Even Harris and Twain doff their outer clothing, dangle their legs in the water,

10. *Writings* 9:107. In the summer of 1891, Twain actually did float down a European river; he bought a flat-bottomed boat and made a ten-day trip down the Rhône, apparently as a remedy for certain feelings of financial desperation. See Kaplan, *Mr. Clemens,* 368–69.

and occasionally go for a swim. However well the fiction of a raft voyage fitted into his plans, this is the only "conveyance" that suggested these contrasts to him. But in the end, this idyllic voyage and the raft itself are disposed of in the same way Twain disposed of Huck and Jim's raft at the end of the first phase of composition of the novel—by a smashup. The raft hit the center pier of a bridge and "went all to smash and scatteration" (164), but for five chapters it had served as an adequate carrier for such anecdotal freight as he cared to bring to it, and the journey evoked an emotional tranquility that contrasted sharply with his own feelings of vexation.

In a later chapter of *A Tramp Abroad,* Twain described the delights of idle traveling and easy companionship, this time in reference to casual walking. "Walking is good to time the movement of the tongue by," he wrote:

> And what a motley variety of subjects a couple of people will casually rake over in the course of a day's tramp! There being no constraint, a change of subject is always in order, and so a body is not likely to keep pegging at a single topic until it grows tiresome. We discussed everything we knew, during the first fifteen or twenty minutes, that morning, and then branched out into the glad, free, boundless realm of the things we were not certain about.[11]

It was precisely this relaxed, associative, speculative mode of creation that Twain did not permit himself when he wrote *Life on the Mississippi* two years later. Evidently, he felt intensely the "constraints" of "pegging at a single topic."

A recent genetic study of this book by Horst H. Kruse modifies the familiar view of *Life on the Mississippi* and, implicitly, of its relation to the composition of *Huckleberry Finn*. The significant relation of *Life on the Mississippi* to *Huckleberry Finn,* unlike that of *A Tramp Abroad,* ought not be sought simply in the recovery of episodes from the completed portion of the novel, nor in the invocation of the dream of drift. To be sure, there are borrowings from the novel: in the clear echoes of *Huckleberry Finn* in chapter 38 ("The House Beautiful"), in

11. *Writings* 9:202–3.

the discussion of southern feuding in chapter 26, and in the direct importation of a segment of the manuscript in chapter 3. However, Kruse has shown that these borrowings do not constitute evidence that the subject of the river impulsively drew Twain back to the pigeonholed manuscript, nor is there evidence that these appropriations were filched from the novel because of flagging invention or the pressure of a contract deadline.[12] Rather, the use of them was calculated well in advance and, except for the directly quoted raft passage of the *Huck Finn* manuscript, they were modified to suit the immediate purpose of the book at hand.

While it may be true, as Kaplan suggests, that the relation of *Life on the Mississippi* to *Huckleberry Finn* was in a sense "symbiotic" and that for Twain the books possessed a certain "overlapping" interest; and while, as William M. Gibson has contended, following Blair, *Life on the Mississippi* "may be regarded as a rich mine for episodes and characters in *Adventures of Huckleberry Finn*," these were, nevertheless, distinctly different books, in character and in conception.[13] It is that very difference that has the most suggestive interest for us here. In fact, Kruse has argued persuasively that *Life on the Mississippi* (except for the earlier "Old Times on the Mississippi" portion) was an altogether different sort of book from the earlier autobiographical works, indeed of a different genre.

From the beginning, Twain strove to write a definitive account of life on the river, a "standard" work as Twain himself had described it, and his return trip to the Mississippi was something of a "field trip" to insure accuracy and objectivity. As a result, he did not speak in the voice of an innocent or a tenderfoot: he adopted an authoritative persona and painstakingly and purposefully supplemented his recent experience on the river by reading and research. He was committed, in short, to pegging away at a single topic, and the genesis of the book shows that the author continually exercised a rational control upon his treatment of the material that checked his

---

12. See Kruse, *Mark Twain and "Life on the Mississippi"* (Amherst: University of Massachusetts Press, 1981), especially chapter 4, "A Summer's Work," 43–91.

13. See Kaplan, *Mr. Clemens,* 289, and Gibson, *The Art of Mark Twain* (New York: Oxford University Press, 1976), 65.

customary and persistent inclination to make for the glad, free realm of speculation and irrelevant anecdote and curtailed his impulse toward random invective and social criticism.[14]

Twain's ambitions for *Life on the Mississippi* were high ones, and his commitment to his original purpose and its completion transcended the simple, nagging obligation of a contract deadline. Nevertheless, he seems to have questioned the value of the authentic and documentary account of river life, even as he was writing it. When an Arkansas traveler brags about the size of his state's mosquitoes, the traveler's friend deflates these exaggerations: "Wait—you are getting that too strong; cut it down, cut it down—you get a leetle too much costumery onto your statements: always dress a fact in tights, never in an ulster. . . . what these gentlemen want for a book is the frozen truth."[15] Rightly or wrongly, Twain was committed for the most part to dressing his "standard" work in tights, and the net effect of this commitment is often an austere, even antiseptic journalism. *Life on the Mississippi* is occasionally fastidious and frequently filled with statistical information—gross revenues of river towns, population increases, and the like—and it gives several pages over to quoting accounts of other Mississippi travelers. But in writing *Life on the Mississippi,* Twain apparently recognized that direct observation and dedication to the "frozen truth" were more often desiccating than vitalizing.

Twain found that a surfeit of experience, however extraordinary, disables the imagination, and he said as much in chapter 35. After enumerating the known facts related to "Vicksburg During the Trouble," he asks, "Could you, who did not experience it, come nearer to reproducing it to the imagination of another non-participant than could a Vicksburger who *did* experience it?" Though it seems impossible, the novel rather than the repeated experience, argues Twain, better outfits the "tongue or pen" for rendering the experience, for it takes a "deathless grip upon his imagination and memory." The first voyage out, the experience "bristles with striking novelties," but by

14. See Kruse, *Mark Twain and "Life,"* especially 5–19.
15. *Life on the Mississippi* (New York: Viking Penguin, 1986), 253.

the tenth "the thing has lost color, snap, surprise; and has become commonplace."[16]

Surely these statements have particular application to his own return to the river after so many years, for he had written "Old Times on the Mississippi" from memory and must have recognized how much more feeling he had put into that than he was able to get into part 2 of *Life on the Mississippi*. He perceived as well that, in contrast to the "grown-up" mask he had adopted for his standard work, with a young and innocent persona all experience may be portrayed as novel, full of color. In chapter 54 ("Past and Present"), Twain walks the streets of Hannibal and spots the house of a boyhood friend: "It carried me back more than a generation in a moment, and landed me in the midst of a time when the happenings of life were not the natural and logical results of great general laws, but of special orders, and were freighted with very precise and distinct purposes—partly punitive in intent, partly admonitory; and usually local in application."[17] Even as he was advancing his theme of progress in *Life on the Mississippi,* he opposed to the universal and statistical the particularizing atmosphere of the youthful imagination that invigorates experience and perception; he was contrasting the world of fact with the world of feeling.

Nor, though devoted to speaking authoritatively about the Mississippi, did he seem to find factual matter the adequate substitute for such feeling. "Emotions are among the toughest things in the world to manufacture out of whole cloth," he wrote; "it is easier to manufacture seven facts than one emotion."[18] This statement is even more revealing when one recognizes that Twain's efforts to collect factual material for his book were by no means always easy and were sometimes frustrating.[19] Life on the river had changed, but so had Mark Twain, and he eventually discovered that his strongest feelings for the Mississippi were wedded to his memory of it and could not be automatically regained by renewed observation. A standard work

16. Ibid., 258, 259.
17. Ibid., 375.
18. Ibid., 198–99.
19. See Kruse, *Mark Twain and "Life,"* 48–53, 58–60.

might possess authority, but it lacked life, and he endorsed the atmospheric vitality of fiction over "frozen truth" when he praised George Washington Cable's *The Grandissimes:* "In him the South has found a masterly delineator of its interior life and its history. In truth, I find by experience, that the untrained eye and vacant mind can inspect it and learn of it and judge of it more clearly and profitably in his books than by personal contact with it."[20] He might have said the same about "Old Times on the Mississippi" or *Huckleberry Finn* itself.

The "difficulties" Twain complained of in writing *Life on the Mississippi,* as Kruse has shown, were not principally related to anxieties over his contractual obligations to finish the book, as had been supposed.[21] One suspects they rather derived from his own, self-imposed constraints to write a standard work, the result of constantly trying to hold in check his impulses to indulge in the peripheral, the anecdotal, the atmospheric, to harness his own strong feelings and maintain an authoritative, dispassionate persona.

Not the least of those feelings was that of moral indignation. Howells had published the first lengthy appreciation of Twain in the *Century Magazine* for September 1882. Twain's humor, he wrote, was "at its best the foamy break of the strong tide of earnestness in him," and he praised the humorist's "indignant sense of right and wrong," his "ardent hate of meanness and injustice."[22] Twain had seen the essay in manuscript as early as June 1882 and had thanked Howells for his evaluation: "I hope the public will be willing to see me with your eyes."[23] And his work in progress provided the occasion to verify Howells's perception of him, for he indulged in some strident social commentary, even though it went against the purpose of a standard work. Twain's recognition of this deviation from his plan (partly pointed out to him by his publisher and partly detected by himself) caused him to temper his moral indignation. Deferring to Osgood's judgment on the point, he deleted two chapters devoted

20. *Life on the Mississippi,* 313.
21. Kruse, *Mark Twain and "Life,"* questions this supposition throughout; see especially chapters 3–4.
22. *Century Magazine* 24.5 (September 1882): 783.
23. 16 June 1882, *Twain–Howells Letters* 1:405.

exclusively to strong social criticism; he muzzled his ardent Republicanism and intense antisouthern feeling, partly to insure, one supposes, that the book might have a market value in the South; he even toned down his familiar, virulent attack on Sir Walter Scott in chapter 46.

In short, Twain seems to have been champing at the bit throughout the composition of *Life on the Mississippi*. No doubt Twain's serious ambitions for his river book and his persistent commitment to an objective detachment contributed to the success of *Life on the Mississippi*, but it was an unfamiliar and stiff collar for him to wear. And it is perhaps significant that when he returned to *Huckleberry Finn* in that last furious burst of composition, he began with Colonel Sherburn's verbal attack on the mob,[24] for in that episode Twain was indulging in his own indignant sense of right and wrong again, and with a vengeance. Though he resumed the mask of Huck shortly after creating that episode, for the moment he would speak through Sherburn, and with the force of personal conviction. In any event, when he returned to the novel, he was no longer under the obligation to peg away at a single subject; he was able to speak for himself, even if he spoke, for the most part, through Huck.

He took up the manuscript of the novel again in the summer or spring of 1883 and wrote with an energy and ease that even he found remarkable; he would "sail right in and sail right on, the whole day long, without thought of running short of stuff or words." The experience was in dramatic contrast to the difficulties he had encountered in writing *Life on the Mississippi*. He had willingly assumed the role of an adult in writing his river book and had attempted to speak rationally and temperately throughout, but Huck's was clearly a more comfortable and artistically satisfying mask for him. "I expect to complete it [*Huckleberry Finn*] in a month or six weeks or two months more," he wrote Howells. "And *I* shall *like* it, whether any-

24. Walter Blair in *Mark Twain and Huck Finn* (Berkeley and Los Angeles: University of California Press, 1960) contends that when Twain threw himself into the novel again in the summer of 1883, he probably began with chapter 22; see 300 and 411 n. 2

body else does or not."[25] He should have liked it, having put so much of himself into it.

III

In September 1884, Twain wrote Howells about the upcoming presidential election: "I only urge you not to soil yourself by voting for Blaine," he advised. "It is not necessary to vote for Cleveland. The only necessary thing to do, as I understand it, is that a man shall keep *himself* clean (by withholding his vote for an improper man) even though the party and the country go to destruction in consequence."[26] He reaffirmed this notion of ethical independence in *A Connecticut Yankee* a few years later when he wrote that a man ought to preserve the single "atom" of self that is worth preserving and let the rest land in "Sheol." Yet when he insisted to Howells that "a man's first duty is to his own honor," Twain was not so much indulging in self-righteousness as he was emulating the moral nature of Huck Finn, who had preserved his own "sound heart" in the face of circumstance and against the claims of his own "deformed conscience" and had promised to "light out for the Territory" to avoid the contaminating effects of "sivilization." The following year, when he came to write "The Private History of a Campaign That Failed," Twain would once again and even more strongly identify himself with Huckleberry Finn.

"The Private History" was printed in *Century Magazine*'s "Battles and Leaders of the Civil War" series in December 1885 and was the first extended piece Twain published after the completion of *Huckleberry Finn.* The author's absorbing interest in his new publishing company, his lecture tour with Cable, and his commercial and personal involvement with Ulysses S. Grant, whose memoirs he had contracted to publish, provided ample preoccupation to divert him

25. *Twain–Howells Letters* 1:435–36.
26. Ibid., 2:508–9

from the now painful business of writing. In view of the fact that these ventures occupied much of his time and taxed his creative energy, his interest in writing his own "war paper" must have been a strong one, and the motives for it may have been several.

In part the piece served in a practical way as advertisement for the Grant *Memoirs*. But, as John Gerber has suggested, Twain's "Campaign" may also have been an effort to justify his own role in the war and was probably prompted by his renewed acquaintance with those familiar with and perhaps disdainful of his military record when he traveled to Hannibal in 1882 and again in 1885. Justin Kaplan believes the story is a symbolic working out of Twain's own complicated relationship with Grant, his feelings for whom sometimes bordered on idolatry.[27] In either case, this "private history" is an attempt at self-vindication on ethical grounds and is more fiction than fact. In a sense, it resembles Melville's "inside narrative" of *Billy Budd* (composed, incidentally, at around the same time), constructed, as it were, from the other side of the cloth. Melville created a fiction that had private reference to and qualified, even if it did not ultimately justify, the recorded conduct of his cousin Guert Gansevoort in the *Somers* mutiny case. Twain, on the other hand, created a "private history," publicly presented as fact, which he must have felt vindicated him of his own questionable conduct during the war and, at the same time, justified his association with the nation's most eminent war hero. Whatever his motives, however strong his pangs of conscience, this invented autobiography, reminiscent of the many "autobiographies" Huck spontaneously manufactures in the novel, represented a symbolic cleansing of the contaminated self. For the first time Twain identified not simply with Huck's free and easy circumstance but with his moral nature as well.

Gerber, who has provided the most thorough analysis of the discrepancies between recorded fact and narrative detail in this memoir, has also identified the multiple parallels between the story and *Huckleberry Finn*. So extensive are the echoes of the novel, in fact, that

27. Gerber, "Mark Twain's 'Private Campaign,'" *Civil War History* 1:37 (March 1955): 37–60; Kaplan, *Mr. Clemens,* 316–25.

Gerber suggested that "in the 'Private History,' Huck becomes Twain."[28] Still, since the fictional details of Huck's life at times displace the autobiographical details of Twain's, one may, without really contradicting Gerber, accept as equally true the converse formulation that Twain became Huck; that, consciously or unconsciously, he enlisted his young outcast to give shape and substance to his own ambiguous experience; in short, that this report on an important phase of the author's history was another instance of life imitating art.

The pattern of action of the "Private History," Gerber observes, "is precisely the pattern which recurs repeatedly in *Huckleberry Finn.* . . . Huck gets into a series of scrapes of increasing complexity and annoyance until finally when matters reach a climax and he can't stand it any longer, he 'lights out.'"[29] From the first sentence, the "Private History" recalls the novel, for Twain strikes an immediately familiar note, though his story is told from the point of view of an outsider, a deserter: "You have heard from a great many people who did something in the war; is it not fair and right that you listen a little moment to one who started out to do something, but didn't?"[30] Though he undertakes to speak for the thousands of like-minded young men who deserted in the early days of the war, Twain assumes a Huck-like pose when he admits that perhaps these men, himself included, ought not be allowed much space "among better people," people who "did something" in the war. Nevertheless, he maintains that even the soldiers who skedaddled ought to be given a chance to explain *why* they didn't do anything. Thus, Twain begins his "war paper" as an effort at self-justification, speaking from the vantage point of a social pariah.

Twain's company, the Marion Rangers, reminds us of Tom Sawyer's band of robbers. Indeed, Gerber notes that the volunteers all talk like Tom, and their leader, Tom Lyman, is constantly urging in Sawyeresque fashion the heedless crew to conform to military custom. One young soldier especially recalls Tom Sawyer's romantic

---

28. "Mark Twain's 'Private Campaign,'" 42.
29. Ibid.
30. *Writings* 15:255.

pretensions. He is described as "young, ignorant, good natured, well-meaning, trivial, full of romance, and given to reading chivalric novels and singing forlorn love-ditties." His "nickel-plated aristocratic instincts" are burlesqued in the opening pages, but Twain describes his own reactions to them in a way that reminds us of what Huck's or Tom's might have been: he thought Peterson Dunlap's giving his own familiar name a French accent "the bravest thing that can be imagined."[31]

On the whole, the young soldiers have little inclination to obey orders, post lookouts, and the like, preferring to indulge in such innocent pastimes as fishing, swimming, smoking, and playing games. These soldiers are more like boys out on a lark than men engaged in the serious business of war. Much like Tom's gang, they react to danger by hiding out and, safe from real conflict, are free to quarrel over the rights and privileges of rank. On one occasion, they lose their guns and a keg of powder scurrying up and down hills in a retreat to the Mason farmhouse. In fact, as Henry Nash Smith has pointed out, this farm itself is reminiscent of the Phelps plantation, though both probably had their emotional origin in the author's memory of the Quarles farm where he often spent his summers as a boy.[32] In any event, like Huck when he arrives at the Phelpses', these soldiers are greeted by several barking dogs, and each one "took a soldier by the slack of the trousers and began to back away with him"; this skirmish, Twain claims, was "perhaps the most terrifying spectacle of the Civil War." The repeated burlesque of their ready impulse to retreat and their undisciplined antics stamps them as a "curious breed of soldiers"; and the upbraiding they receive from the "grown up" Mr. Mason makes them feel "shabbier than the dogs had done."[33]

Despite their wounded dignity and bruised feet, war for them is more a welcome escape from responsibility and routine than a call to duty. "For a time," wrote Twain, "life was idly delicious, it was

31. Ibid., 257.
32. *Mark Twain: The Development of a Writer* (New York: Atheneum, 1967), 130–31.
33. *Writings* 15:268, 269.

perfect, there was nothing to mar it."[34] Their "holiday" is peri-
odically interrupted by retreats, but, however discomfiting these
may have actually been, Twain's description of his several flights
from the enemy in this memoir possesses nothing of that "hard
baked" familiarity with feelings of "death-on-a-pale-horse-with-
hell-following-after" that he confessed to in a letter to an uniden-
tified correspondent in 1890.[35] Rather, as the multiple parallels
between this history and *Huckleberry Finn* indicate, Twain, once
again, was recovering from his novel the mood of an easy and free
existence.

However, the essential relation between *Huckleberry Finn* and this
autobiographical piece is somewhat different from that between the
novel and either *A Tramp Abroad* or *Life on the Mississippi,* because
here Twain seems not to have simply envied Huck's easy circumstance but to have identified with his natural sympathies as well.
This difference signals a shift in the basis of Twain's identification
with his created character. For it was not nostalgia that drew him
toward his subject and prompted his importation of Huck into his
autobiography. If anything, Twain was dredging up bad memories,
not fond ones. Under the circumstances, his published account of
this episode in his life invited public scorn. But Twain saved his war
paper from becoming pure burlesque and, to a degree, justified his
behavior during the war when he provided his own adventures with
a significant dramatic climax, almost surely a fabrication,[36] and described his moral revulsion in a way that linked him to his fictional
character.

The nervousness created by rumors of enemy troops in the area
causes the undisciplined soldiers to fire precipitately at a man who
happens to ride past their encampment in Mr. Mason's barn one
night, and the Rangers watch the man gasp out his dying breath:
"The thought shot through me that I was a murderer, that I had
killed a man—a man who had never done me any harm. That was

34. Ibid., 266.
35. Reprinted in *The Portable Mark Twain,* ed. Bernard DeVoto (New York: Viking
Press, 1946), 773–75.
36. See Gerber, "Mark Twain's 'Private Campaign,'" 42, on this point.

the coldest sensation that ever went through my marrow." Even as the narrator regards the dying man with "pitying interest," his conscience begins to gnaw at him: "my imagination persuaded me that the dying man gave me a reproachful look out of his shadowy eyes, and it seemed to me that I would rather he had stabbed me than done that." The thought of this dying man "preys" upon him every night. This senseless killing, he decides, was "an epitome of war." His campaign was "spoiled," and he resolved to "retire from this vocation of sham soldiership while I could save some remnant of my self-respect."[37] His desertion, we are to understand, is not the shirking of duty but the attempt to keep himself "clean" and is prompted by the introduction of the sort of dramatic incident that Melville in *Billy Budd* called a "moral emergency."

It is not so much that this invented shooting resembles any particular episode in *Huckleberry Finn* (though the dying man's outspread arms, bloody front, and gasping breaths recall the Boggs killing, and Twain's reaction to it resembles Huck's reaction to Buck Grangerford's death). The significance instead lies in the dramatization of a certain revulsion of feeling that Huck had had throughout the novel, especially in the latter half. Nor, for that matter, was it necessary for Twain to resort to this strategy to exonerate his conduct during the war. As Gerber has pointed out, Twain made explicit certain common and understandable reasons why a young man in Missouri might have deserted the army during the early days of the war. Like many new recruits at the time, Twain had mixed loyalties, which, coupled with his own lack of training and discipline, created in him an ambivalence, if not a genuine moral confusion. Twain was not the only soldier to desert under similar conditions. But these constituted complicating and extenuating circumstances that, though they might *excuse* his behavior, could not *sanctify* it. What was missing was a demonstration of innate and superior moral impulses, what Thomas Jefferson had called a "generous spasm of the heart." Walter Blair has observed, "For all his talk about believing man 'merely a machine automatically functioning,' Mark had not been completely converted

37. *Writings* 15:277–79.

by his own eloquence."[38] In opposition to his announced cynicism, he had attributed to Huck a "sound heart," and in the "Private History" had appropriated it as his own.

The bouts Twain has with his conscience (what he calls in the "Private History" the "diseased imagination") are of the same sort Huck has in the novel. His overwrought and, to a degree, unwarranted display of guilt, as Smith notes, reminds us of Huck's feelings of blame when he sees the tarred and feathered king and duke: "it don't make no difference whether you do right or wrong, a person's conscience ain't got no sense, and just goes for him *anyway*. If I had a yaller dog that didn't know no more than a person's conscience does, I would pison him. It takes up more room than all the rest of a person's insides, and yet ain't no good, nohow" (290). While he pretends to recognize the legitimacy of this killing as the unfortunate but natural consequence of a nation at war, his sympathies run in the opposite direction: "He was killed in war; killed in fair and legitimate war; killed in battle, as you may say; and yet he was as sincerely mourned by the opposing force as if he had been their brother." His resolution to quit soldiering is attended by some feelings of guilt, to be sure, but it is the kind of compromised guilt Huck has about his "sinfulness" in helping Jim escape: "It seemed to me that I was not rightly equipped for this awful business; that war was intended for men, and I for a child's nurse" (279). He would take up the wicked business of desertion, for he was not "brung up" to the bloody business of war. However, one may judge from his characterization of those who stayed in the army that the proper "equipment" for war is a callous, desperate, even sinister quality that though "manly" by society's reckoning, was at odds with his own natural, if childlike, sympathies.

In essence, Twain invested his own life with the ethical superiority he had supplied his young outcast. There is no evidence that Twain later remembered this fictionalized killing as a real occurrence, as he apparently remembered coming within a "few hours" and a "few miles" of meeting Grant on the battlefield, though he and

38. *Mark Twain and Huck Finn,* 343.

Grant had together determined their close call was nearer twenty-five miles and two weeks.[39] But the net effect of this alteration of autobiographical detail was that he rewrote his own life in terms of his fiction, identified his own character with Huck's. It is a matter of record that Twain himself "lit out for the territory" only a week or two after he quit the Marion Rangers, though his trip was probably more a search for opportunity than a blameless escape from the contaminating circumstance of public responsibility and "siviliza-tion." Several years after he wrote "The Private History," Twain insisted to Kipling that a "joggle to circumstance" would alter the fundamental nature of Tom Sawyer, make of him either an "angel or a rip" as his creator saw fit.[40] It was just such a "joggle" to the details of his own life that must have made Twain, in his own mind at least, a fit companion to share with Grant the national prominence and es-teem that both enjoyed so many years after the war and that verified Howells's assessment of him as a moral spokesman for the times, a view Twain hoped the public would share. Whatever the nature of Twain's private feelings concerning his war record, his published account of it provided him with a sound heart that triumphed over his deformed conscience. Though the "Private History" ends in bur-lesque, Twain had turned to the fiction of *Huckleberry Finn* to give his memoir its emotional center and its shape. But, then, he had been there before.

39. As Kaplan points out (*Mr. Clemens,* 312–22), Twain was fascinated by the possibility that he and Grant had come close to facing each other on the battlefield. Shortly after Grant had established that they had missed each other by a few weeks, Twain recorded in his notebook that their possible meeting was separated by "a day or two," and his published memoir brought them even closer together.

40. Reported in DeLancey Ferguson, *Mark Twain, Man and Legend* (New York: Charter Books, 1963), 241–42.

"LEARNING A NIGGER TO ARGUE"
Quitting *Huckleberry Finn*

I

THERE ARE TWO CONCLUSIONS to the *Adventures of Huckleberry Finn*. The first is the narrative conclusion that, among other things, announces the depletion of the narrator's materials for this makeshift tale carved out of his "adventures." We are to believe that Huck is genuinely relieved that there "ain't nothing more to write about" (362). He informs us that he will likely "light out" for the Territory to avoid the "sivilizing" efforts of Aunt Sally and generously bids us all farewell with "THE END. YOURS TRULY, HUCK FINN." Getting out of the "trouble" of the making of a book is easy enough for Huck—unfitted for the task, he simply gives it up and moves on. The second conclusion is Twain's own private and inconspicuous exit from the novel, his own giving up and moving on to other adventures. It is with this second conclusion that we are here concerned because it offers a glimpse of Twain's ethical and imaginative investment in his novel and in his created characters, and it urges upon us a certain kind of speculation about the author's special difficulties in satisfactorily finishing his book.

Smuggled into Twain's story of Huckleberry Finn were two and a half chapters of interpolated material. A portion of this material represents the author's final efforts at what he had described seven years earlier in a letter to Howells as "Huck Finn's Autobiography."

At least seventeen manuscript pages of these chapters appear to constitute Twain's private conclusion to the book. If Huck had no more to write about, Twain, it seems, did, for he added the "King Sollermun" episode after Huck's tale ended, and with little apparent narrative purpose.[1]

The first, or narrative, conclusion muddies the waters of formal criticism of the novel as novel, and it has excited long-standing and familiar critical debate. It is, in the current critical idiom, a "closure" that devilishly opens onto indefinite, perhaps infinite, critical interpretation. Yet Huck and Tom's "evasion" has an interesting parallel in Mark Twain's own personal evasion of a problem with his novel, for the second, or compositional, conclusion is more precisely a "quitting" than anything else. Less than a farewell to the reader, it is the author's own farewell to a book that had engaged his creative imagination more profoundly and more intensely than any of his other works.

The author's ambivalent and perhaps confused relation to *Huckleberry Finn* is significant because it provokes several questions about Twain and his book and invites a degree of speculation about the nature of the author's complicated involvement with his story and his emotional identification not only with his title character, but also with the slave Jim. "Nigger Jim" is one of Twain's most interesting creations, and Twain's difficulties with him pose some intriguing questions which are not entirely unrelated to recent complaints that *Adventures of Huckleberry Finn* is a racist book. Though in the following pages it may seem that I reason too minutely on the event, the last two sentences Twain wrote in *Huckleberry Finn* are, I think, especially suggestive of his complex attitudes toward Jim and, by

---

1. Walter Blair, in *Mark Twain and Huck Finn* (Berkeley and Los Angeles: University of California Press, 1960), writes, "Two narrative sketches completed the book, an insertion telling about the visit of Huck and Jim to the wrecked *Walter Scott,* the talk with the ferry boat owner, and the arguments about King Solomon and the French language" (346). Elsewhere, Blair and Hamlin Hill note that "the *Walter Scott* episode . . . and the discussion about Solomon and the French language were crammed into their places in 1883, and the book was complete" (*The Art of Huckleberry Finn* [San Francisco: Chandler Publishing Co., 1962], 7).

implication, toward the Negro, and they are therefore deserving of some special attention.

Twain's bit of self-parody about viewing the masterpieces in *A Tramp Abroad* might serve as an instructive parable for contemporary critics. Everything about Bassano's painting *Pope Alexander III and the Doge Ziani,* including its title, Twain jested, served to divert attention from its true subject and its true achievement—a hair trunk. The "soul" of Bassano's painting exists in this hair trunk, however much its refinements are obscured: "Some of the effects are very daring, approaching even to the boldest flights of the rococo, the sirocco, and the Byzantine schools . . . and with that art which conceals art."[2] I am less interested here in Twain's art than in his motives as an artist, and those motives may be concealed in even so slight a detail as a hair trunk, provided that detail represents a larger impulse. Grandiose claims have been made for that moment Twain decided to begin *Huckleberry Finn* (all of modern American literature derives from it, we are told). My own claims are far less grand, but there is at least something interesting and curious about the way Twain ended his book.

When Mark Twain returned to the *Huck Finn* manuscript for the last time in the summer of 1883, he was in a lynching mood. He had muzzled his anger with the damned human race, and more particularly with the South, in the writing of *Life on the Mississippi,* but he spoke his mind clearly and directly when he took up the novel again with chapter 22.[3] There, the indignant Colonel Sherburn mocks his would-be lynchers, and it is through Sherburn rather than Huck that Twain voices his contempt for the South and the cowardice of mobs. Twain had his opportunity to lynch Sherburn for the cold-blooded killing of Boggs, but apparently his disdain for the mob outstripped his contempt for southern aristocracy. Nevertheless, he seems to have contemplated lynching *somebody* throughout the final phase of composition of the novel.

2. *A Tramp Abroad* (Hartford, Conn.: American Publishing Co., 1880), 566.

3. See Blair, *Mark Twain and Huck Finn,* 300 and 411 n. 2. I have discussed elsewhere some of the implications of Twain's adoption of Sherburn as the voice of his own indignation in "Life Imitating Art: *Huckleberry Finn* and Twain's Autobiographical Writings" above.

Even earlier, in his working notes for the novel, Twain twice jotted down notes for episodes that might be included. In Group A of the working notes he had merely written the reminder, "A lynching scene";[4] later, in Group C, he had written "They [presumably a southern mob] lynch a free nigger." In chapter 30 Huck contrives to have the king and duke believe that he has given them the slip for fear of being hanged. The possibility is real enough, and the duke observes that if luck had not been on their side, "we'd a slept in our cravats to-night—cravats warranted to *wear,* too—longer than *we'd* need 'em" (262). And in the penultimate chapter of *Huckleberry Finn,* with the return of the wounded Tom and the capture of Jim, Huck records that the "huffy" captors wanted to lynch Jim as "an example to all the other niggers around there" (352). But they give up the project because Jim is undoubtedly another man's property and those "that's always most anxious for to hang a nigger that hain't done just right, is always the very ones that ain't the most anxious to pay for him when they've got their satisfaction out of him" (352).

Surely Huck's observation here serves as ironic commentary on Twain's earlier note—for the only thing that protects Jim's life and liberty in the South, it appears, is the mistaken belief that he is a slave and therefore a white man's property. Nevertheless, there is the interesting and disturbing possibility that Twain had considered concluding his book with the lynching of Jim (the only "free nigger" in the book except for the "white-shirted" one Pap rails against, a man surely too smart to find himself in Arkansas), and that final punishment after the humiliations he had already suffered at the hands of Huck and Tom. Had he done so, Twain might have produced one of the darkest, most nihilistic books in all of American fiction. Had Twain made his Nigger Jim a Nigger Jeff, surely no one would be able to argue that the evasion episode represents a moral retreat on Twain's part had he followed it, as the clear and direct extension of the attitude embodied in the childish romanticism of Tom Sawyer, with

4. Bernard DeVoto, *Mark Twain at Work* (Cambridge: Harvard University Press, 1942), 67. DeVoto's organization of the working notes is discussed in detail in "Nobility out of Tatters: The Writing of *Huckleberry Finn*" above.

a real lynching. Even so, Twain cannot be charged with indifference or ignorance about the racist nature of the evasion episode, for he later pointed out in *Tom Sawyer, Detective,* after Uncle Silas is imprisoned, that a white man would not let Huck and Tom "break him out of prison the way we done with our old nigger Jim."[5]

Mark Twain's quarrel with the South was deep and intense, and he felt his own southern origins as a humiliation.[6] But he divided his contempt for southern backwater behavior between dramatizing its cruelty on the one hand and its cowardice on the other. And it is southern cowardice that saves both Sherburn and Jim from being lynched, though the former is certainly a deserving candidate for such attention even if the latter is not. Nevertheless, part of Twain's problem with finishing his book, I would argue, was his indecision about what to do with Jim, and it was a problem that had its sources less in his frustration about narrative invention than in his own difficulty with what his friend George Washington Cable called the "Negro question." When Twain first decided to set his manuscript of *Huckleberry Finn* aside, he, in evident frustration with the way his story was developing, had a steamboat knock Huck's raft "all to flinders"; he might have solved the problem with Jim similarly by lynching him, by simply eliminating him.

But he did not. Instead, he wrote the King Solomon episode, which constitutes most of chapter 14, as his last contribution to the novel. The last words of that episode, and therefore, except for later revisions, the last words Mark Twain wrote in *Huckleberry Finn,* are: "you can't learn a nigger to argue. So I quit" (98). How apt is that final sentence. It signals Twain's despair over the intellectual limitations of his characters and his own exhaustion of creative energies. Twain had wrestled with the book for nearly a decade, and though the final

5. *The Adventures of Tom Sawyer, Tom Sawyer Abroad, and Tom Sawyer, Detective,* vol. 6 of *The Works of Mark Twain,* foreword and notes by John Gerber, text established by Paul Baender (Berkeley and Los Angeles: University of California Press, 1980), 411.

6. Twain's shifting and ambivalent reactions to the South are sensitively traced in Arthur Gordon Pettit's *Mark Twain and the South* (Lexington: University of Kentucky Press, 1974).

phase of composition was written at high pitch and with exhilarating satisfaction, Walter Blair has noted that Twain was tiring and the book was a "tough one to finish and he was postponing the end."[7]

Mark Twain simply quit his book, and the remark "So I quit" appears to be an afterthought—the three words are crammed into the lower right-hand corner of the manuscript page, an emblem that represents Twain's own frustrations as much as they do Huck's, albeit in a very different way.

II

Extant evidence suggests that the King Solomon episode was written separately. The manuscript pages are numbered one through seventeen and were later corrected to conform with the pagination of the manuscript of the novel as a whole. Ironically, the episode begins after the paragraph in which Jim recites his fear for his situation when he discovers that the raft has become unmoored from the grounded *Walter Scott*. Jim instantly recognizes his difficulty. If he doesn't drown, he will be saved; and if he is saved, he will be returned upriver to Miss Watson, only to be sold downriver in turn, a fate comparable to and perhaps worse than death. Huck's reaction to this line of reasoning contrasts sharply with his concluding remarks at the end of the chapter: "Well, he was right; he was most always right; he had an uncommon level head, for a nigger" (93). Huck's belief in Jim's levelheadedness, on the one hand, and his equal belief in Jim's natural, racial incapacity for argument, on the other, constitute the terms of Twain's own befuddlement about Jim. Twain had little difficulty in dramatizing Jim's instinctive shrewdness and native intelligence, but Jim's possibilities as a character who might argue beyond his immediate circumstance seem remote and implausible.[8] Yet however erroneous and amusing Jim's argument in

7. See *Mark Twain and Huck Finn*, 350.
8. As David L. Smith notes in "Huck, Jim, and American Racial Discourse," *Mark*

the King Solomon episode may be, his reasoning is far more rigorous and logically consistent than Huck's.

The genesis of this episode derived from the need to satisfy three possible strands of narrative development Twain recorded in his working notes. All of these occur in the last, Group C section. In one of these notes Twain had written "Back yonder, Huck reads & tells about monarchies & kings &c. So Jim stares when he learns the rank of these 2 [the Duke and Dauphin]."[9] Bernard DeVoto points out that "Mark had decided to introduce the king and the duke, and so invented the wrecked *Walter Scott* in order to provide Huck with books of history he could read to Jim." He further maintains that the King Solomon portion of chapter 14 contains "the reason for the whole [*Walter Scott*] episode," or chapters 13, 14, and most of chapter 12.[10] This is unconvincing for several reasons. First, the King Solomon episode was written independently and, according to Blair, the *Walter Scott* episode was probably written prior to the Phelps chapters and therefore was separated in time as well as in his imagination. Second, the floating house of chapter 9 provided Huck and Jim with such diverse "truck" that Twain could have revised that chapter easily enough and have tossed in a book or two of history—he had given them a "seedy old chest" and an "old hair trunk" (62), both of which were nearly empty, and at least had room for a few books. Third, the episode, if anything, ultimately reveals Jim's clear-eyed skepticism about the right of kings and the wisdom of monarchs rather than open-mouthed credulity. For he imagines Solomon victimized by the domestic racket of a harem, pities unskilled royalty who come to America and can find no "situation," and is angered by the notion that the Frenchman "doan' . . . *talk* like a man" (98). Blair, on the other hand, advances the more plausible argument that Twain

---

Twain Journal 22 (Fall 1984): "While Jim's response—that a man should talk like a man—betrays his ignorance of cultural diversity, his argument is perceptive and structurally sound. The humor in Huck's conclusion, 'you can't learn a nigger how [*sic*] to argue,' arises precisely from our recognition that Jim's argument is better than Huck's" (8).

9. DeVoto, *Mark Twain at Work*, 75.

10. Ibid., 62.

wished to repeat "motifs with variations" in his book and that portray-
ing the cruelty of a real robber gang soon after his portrayal of Tom's
band of pirates provided such a parallel.[11] However, this makes the
King Solomon episode all the more curious because, by itself, it does
nothing to contribute to this parallelism. If Twain had Jim lynched,
as he seems to have considered doing, however, he would have provided a devastating parallel to the near lynching of Colonel Sherburn.

Another note is also related to the Solomon episode: "Takes history class among the niggers?"[12] The note is itself ambiguous. Perhaps, as DeVoto believed, Twain contemplated having Huck teach
history to a group of Negroes. Surely, given Twain's typical treatment of the other blacks in the novel, this was a germ for burlesque
humor in which the Negroes would serve as darkie comic figures
whose reactions, like Jim's, would be bug-eyed disbelief, but without
Jim's sensible rejoinders. Still a third note suggests another strand of
potential dramatic development. Twain considered dramatizing a
scene of "very religious" Arkansas women, knitting and spitting and
gossiping. "Let em drop in ignorant remarks about monarchs in Europe," he wrote, "& mix them up with Biblical monarchs."[13] Louis
Budd believes that Twain's "distaste for fundamentalism guided the
fooling about Solomon's thousand wives," and, by implication, that
Twain might smuggle in his scorn for fundamentalist ignorance and
false gentility by putting it in the mouth of a Negro.[14] And Budd is
no doubt right as well in saying that, all in all, Twain's attitude
toward the Negro is not very admirable, that he, in fact, "pandered to
the sense of innate white superiority still felt in nearly every quarter" of the nation in as recent a work as *Life on the Mississippi*.[15] Yet it
should be added that Twain had used the black character often and
early as a goad to white pretense and gentility as well.

As early as 1864 Twain had satirically questioned the propriety

11. Blair, *Mark Twain and Huck Finn,* 347.
12. DeVoto, *Mark Twain at Work,* 75.
13. Ibid., 76.
14. *Mark Twain: Social Philosopher* (Bloomington: Indiana University Press, 1962),
104.
15. Ibid., 105.

and motives of the good ladies of Carson City, Nevada, who had given a charity ball to raise money for the "Sanitary Fund" (the Civil War's equivalent to the Red Cross).[16] Twain wrote in his *Enterprise* column that there was some question whether the proceeds would actually go to the Sanitary Fund or, instead, to a Miscegenation Society somewhere back East. The jest resulted in a public outcry and nearly resulted in a duel. To provide only one other example, we might note that many years later, Twain, perhaps with similar mischief in mind, allowed that he supposed it common knowledge that the Virgin Mary was a black woman.[17]

The comic possibilities of the black character constituted a double-edged sword: he might be used conventionally as the butt of a joke, as a minstrel figure; on the other hand, the shallowness and ignorance of white society might be effectively lampooned by the wry use of that same conventional bias against the Negro. Indeed, Twain in the transparent guise of "Misto C." made himself the butt of just such a joke in the moving sketch "A True Story," where his own failure to recognize the common and real emotional nature of the black Aunt Rachel is ridiculed. These examples are perhaps sufficient to show Twain's other use of the Negro as satirical vehicle rather than satirical object. Surely Huck's avowal, at the conclusion of the King Solomon episode, that you can't "learn a nigger to argue" is analogous in substance and intent, for Jim has just won the argument hands down.

These three germinal strands for dramatic incident were nicely woven together in the episode that eventually resulted, though in ways that seem to satisfy no single artistic intention suggested by the separate notes, nor all three at once. Twain's contempt for fundamentalism is so cloaked in burlesque as to constitute, if anything, a very private though perhaps personally gratifying joke. Given Huck's misshapen historical sense (he plays Tom to Jim's Huck in this scene), whatever Twain had in mind when he contemplated a "history class

16. Reported in Delancey Fergusson's *Mark Twain: Man and Legend* (New York: Bobbs Merrill Co., 1943), 93.
17. Reported in *The Crisis: A Record of the Darker Races,* May 1912, 20.

among the niggers" is not fulfilled in the incident as it stands; surely it fails to burlesque the ignorance of Negroes as a race. And, as already observed, Jim's reaction to the king and duke in chapter 19 is hardly prepared for by the Solomon episode.

The question then remains: Why did Twain feel impelled to insert this brief incident after the novel was essentially complete? And it is a question further complicated by the special satisfaction he took in the episode. After the completion of *Huckleberry Finn,* Twain went on an extended lecture tour with George Washington Cable. Twain, if he sometimes resented his fastidiousness, nevertheless admired Cable's moral courage and especially his bold arguments for full civil rights for the Negro, arguments that resulted in denunciations and threats, particularly from his native South. Cable's views on race and race prejudice were well known; Twain's, if as strong, were ambiguous, and ambiguously stated.

During the lecture tour, Twain obviously wished to advertise his forthcoming novel, the first to be published by his newly formed publishing company. His personal stakes in and expectations for "Huck Finn's Autobiography" were high. And the portion of the novel he read from most often (in fact, one of his most frequent lecture offerings on that tour) was "How come a Frenchman doan' . . . *talk* like a man?" or the King Solomon episode.[18] Whatever other reasons he may have had, his decision to read this portion of the book would have satisfied an unlikely dilemma. Obliged on the one hand to play the role of the nation's funny man, and thus to present to the public an appetizing foretaste of the humor of his latest novel, he must have felt the pains of whatever demeaning ingratiation normally attends such self-advertisement.[19] On the other hand, he was probably impelled to present (at least to his own, private satisfaction) a version of himself as morally courageous about the Negro question as he thought Cable to be. An analogous dilemma pre-

18. See Paul Fatout, *Mark Twain on the Lecture Circuit* (Bloomington: Indiana University Press, 1960), 215.

19. Twain complained that his stage antics on this tour made a "buffoon" of him, that the experience was "demeaning," even "ghastly." See Fatout, *Mark Twain on the Lecture Circuit,* 221.

sented itself when he became professionally associated with the nation's Civil War hero, Ulysses S. Grant. For a deserter, the association
was an awkward one, and he seems to have solved it in a way by writing
"The Private History of a Campaign That Failed," wherein he justified his behavior in several ways, but mostly by representing himself
as one who was not "made" for the business of war; for he presented
himself as possessing a natural aversion to cruelty and killing.[20]

At any rate, there is little evidence that Twain thought the King
Solomon episode farcical, though he no doubt recognized its humor.
Walter Blair finds this interlude "minstrel-show stuff which does
little to develop the book's theme."[21] Yet the episode has a special
sort of poignancy. Jim despises King Solomon, whom he knows "by
de back," because he supposes him to be wasteful of his multitude of
children—"You take a man dat's got on'y one er two chillen' is dat
man gwyne to be waseful o' chillen? No, he ain't; he can't 'ford it.
He know how to value 'em" (96). Huck tells Jim that the son of Louis
XVI, the "boy dolphin," had been imprisoned, and Jim's reaction is
the simple "Po' little chap" (96). Jim is similarly sympathetic when
Huck tells him that some believe the boy escaped to America because Jim recognizes that a king could get no "situation" in this
country. In short, Jim reasons by his own lights in this episode and
responds to Huck's history lesson out of a profound feeling for or
sensitivity to family, imprisonment, and employment.

If Twain saw fit to represent his forthcoming novel to the public
by this episode, it may be that in his own mind it somehow bore the
weight of the whole novel. After the humiliation Jim had suffered,
due in part to the prankish behavior of Tom Sawyer, with Huck as
his nerveless accomplice, and after the cuffing, near lynching, and
chaining by his adult captors, Twain gave to Jim as yet undramatized
capacities that at once rounded out his full humanity and deepened
his tragedy.

As is often the case with him, Twain achieved his realism in the

---

20. This episode in Twain's life is discussed in Justin Kaplan's *Mr. Clemens and
Mark Twain: A Biography* (New York: Simon and Schuster, 1966), 274–77.

21. Blair, *Mark Twain and Huck Finn,* 348–49.

creation of Nigger Jim by a sort of mean averaging. If Jim is super-
stitious, he also has a transcendent understanding of the workings of
man and nature. If he is obsequious, he also gives Huck a tongue
lashing that so affects the boy that he "humbles" himself to Jim in
chapter 15. If Jim is capable of legitimate sympathy, even for the Tom
Sawyer who would have put rattlesnakes in his cell, he was, by his
own account, capable of unthinking cruelty to his own deaf daughter. If he is heroic in helping the doctor tend to the wounded Tom
Sawyer, he is a craven aboard the *Walter Scott*. Jim is a fully human-
ized character because, as Ralph Ellison has observed, "he, like all
men, is ambiguous, limited in circumstance but not in possibility."[22]

The King Solomon episode invests Jim with an intellectual curiosity
and penetration (however erroneous his understanding of the world
apart from his local experience of it may be). It is this human capacity
that rounds out Jim's character, but it is also this feature of Jim's
personality that Huck fails to perceive. Huck eventually recognizes
Jim's capacity for love and attachment to family, his righteous indignation, his self-sacrifice. But Huck never quite understands Jim's capacity
to reason and to argue. There is a special irony here because Huck is so
often characterized as a little pragmatist whose judgments about the
"real" are a humorous and biting version of the "radically empirical."
Jim's intelligence is acute and his sympathies comprehensive, but he
has been culturally deprived. He lacks an understanding of history and
the world that reaches beyond immediate experience. However humorous it may be that Jim is genuinely surprised that the Frenchman
does not speak like a man, his evident "stupidity" is due to a cultural
inheritance that has been withheld from him.

III

The dimensions of Jim's character cannot be entirely attributed to
close observation or to his creator's announced "appreciation" for

22. "Twentieth-Century Fiction and the Black Mask of Humanity," in *Shadow and
Act* (New York: New American Library, 1966), 49.

the "finest qualities" of blacks that he had acquired as a child on the Quarles farm. As Arthur Pettit has convincingly shown, Twain, the man, was only a partly reconstructed southerner, and he never completely outlived his earliest impressions of the Negro.[23] The record of Twain's own racial prejudice is too complete to make of him an enlightened, wholly unbiased champion of blacks. To do so would be as grave an error as it would be to make Huck Finn into an unwashed, adolescent political liberal. Those who champion or condemn Mark Twain's racial views on the basis of his biography and who, in turn, praise or blame *Huckleberry Finn,* somehow miss the point. It was Mark Twain, imaginative artist, not Samuel Clemens, U.S. citizen, who wrote *Huckleberry Finn.* While it is true that Samuel Clemens paid a young black man's tuition at Yale, it is also true that he often complained about the inferiority of Negroes in letters to his mother. Mark Twain, the artist, imagined and created Nigger Jim, but as a man he too was limited by circumstance, but not by possibility.

Twain possessed a double imaginative talent, at once projective and assimilative. And, if we are to trust Rhett Jones on the point, he also possessed a white "double-consciousness" that enabled Twain to see Jim at one moment as a human being, at another as a "nigger." At all events, we can agree with Jones that it is "profitless" to argue about whether or not he was a racist.[24] The authenticity of Jim as a literary creation does not exclusively depend upon Twain's social consciousness, any more than it does upon his acquaintance with the life of the Negro. The degree of Twain's familiarity with black folkways, dialect, behavior, and so forth has been adequately inquired into. But the creative sources for whatever achievement there is in the creation of Jim ought to be sought in the creator's basis of identification with his character rather than in his acquaintance with

23. See Pettit's "Mark Twain, Unreconstructed Southerner, and His View of the Negro, 1835–1860," *The Rocky Mountain Social Science Journal* 7 (1970): 16–27; "Mark Twain and the Negro, 1867–1869," *The Journal of Negro History* 56 (April 1971): 88–96; and *Mark Twain and the South,* passim, especially 123–38, 157–73.

24. "Nigger and Knowledge: White Double Consciousness in *Adventures of Huckleberry Finn,*" *Mark Twain Journal* 20 (Fall 1984): 36.

blacks as subject matter. So completely and successfully did Twain "imagine" Jim that Ralph Ellison might claim that after *Huckleberry Finn* "the Negro generally disappears from fiction as a rounded human being."[25]

Ellison, it is true, attributes this achievement as much to historical circumstance as to literary genius. For Twain wrote at a time when a black character might serve in America as a kind of Everyman, one whose personal fate implicated the nation at large. Nevertheless, it is worth noting Ellison's belief (recorded in 1953) that no writer, white or black, before or since, ever quite rendered a black character in so significant a way. Nor is Ellison alone among blacks in his praise of the book. Despite recent and rather strident objections to the "racism" of *Huckleberry Finn,* the prevailing view of a group of black scholars and critics expressed in a special issue of the *Mark Twain Journal* is that the novel is a powerfully antiracist book. One critic, in fact, maintains that, "except for Melville's work, *Huckleberry Finn* is without peers among major Euro-American novels for its explicitly anti-racist stance."[26]

The sources of this stance, as I say, ought not to be sought in Twain's private or public views about race. With the possible exception of his creation of Roxy in *Pudd'nhead Wilson,* Twain's portrayal of Jim is unexampled in his canon. There is no way around the fact. And Jim was figured forth by Twain's creative imagination, not his political conscience, for that is the way of art. To create such a character required that his creation be developed from within rather than from without. But Twain's special success with Jim may be clarified by a brief rehearsal of his failures.

Often enough, Twain flinched when he treated racial subjects, his own powerful bias dislodging his moral convictions. Here are two examples. On August 23, 1877, Twain witnessed a remarkable act of heroism on the part of a black man. A runaway buggy carrying Ida Langdon, Livy's sister-in-law, was rushing toward a cliff. A middle-aged Negro, John T. Lewis, threw himself at the horse and stopped

---

25. "Twentieth-Century Fiction and the Black Mask of Humanity," 11.
26. Smith, "Huck, Jim, and American Racial Discourse," 4.

the carriage very near the cliff. This is the stuff of melodrama and rich in literary possibility. Twain was deeply affected by the event and tried several times to work it into a fictional narrative. The closest he came to publishing a fictionalized version of the event occurred in *Simon Wheeler,* but in that fiction he made the hero of the episode white, not black. He did dramatize just such an episode in *Pudd'nhead Wilson,* where he had the huge Negro slave Jasper stop a runaway carriage. But Twain got cold feet and deleted the incident from the published book.[27]

He had also flinched in the same novel with the portrayal of Tom's confused recognition that he is black. Tom hates the blacks as "niggers" and hates himself for being one. Yet he hates the whites even more for making him hate himself. His hatred is as intense as it is confused, and his emotional complex is akin to that identified by so many black writers of the twentieth century.[28] The published dramatization of this psychic condition would have to wait for the likes of a Richard Wright or a Ralph Ellison, a James Baldwin or an Eldridge Cleaver, for Twain deleted these passages from his novel as well.

Nor did Twain do any better by Jim in his other Huck and Tom books—*Huck Finn and Tom Sawyer among the Indians* (unpublished) and *Tom Sawyer Abroad* (1894). In both, Twain invests Jim with a practical and realistic skepticism about Tom's romantic pretensions, but in neither does Jim make anything more than a casual and deferential rejoinder. In the first novel, Jim questions Tom's romanticized view of the Indian, but soon after Jim is kidnapped. Had he finished it, *Huck and Tom among the Indians* would have likely included a second evasion episode, this time with feathers and warpaint. In *Tom Sawyer Abroad* Jim is also deferential to "Mars Tom," and Twain was content to express Jim's reactions to Tom's romanticism by lassitude rather than logic.

In one of the more amusing episodes of *Tom Sawyer Abroad,* Twain

27. Recorded in Robert Rowlette's *Mark Twain's "Pudd'nhead Wilson": The Development and Design* (Bowling Green: Bowling Green University Press, 1971), 8–9.

28. See Daniel Morley McKeithan, "The Morgan Manuscript of Mark Twain's *Pudd'nhead Wilson,*" in *Essays and Studies on American Language and Literature,* no. 12 (Cambridge: Harvard University Press, 1961), especially 61–64.

has Tom undertake to instruct Jim in the use of moral "lessons." The moral lesson is ultimately useless, argues Tom, "because the thing don't ever happen the same way again—and can't. The time Hen Scovil fell down the chimbly and crippled his back for life, everybody said it would be a lesson to him. What kind of lesson? How was he going to use it? He couldn't climb chimblies no more, and he hadn't no more backs to break." Jim's mild rejoinder is, "All de same, Mars Tom, dey *is* sich a thing as learnin' by expe'ence." But Tom persists. He cites his Uncle Abner's wisdom that "a person that started in to carry a cat home by the tail was gitting knowledge that was always going to be useful to him, and warn't ever going to grow dim or doubtful."[29] As Tom waxes eloquent, Jim becomes sleepy and finally dozes off. The scene is amusing, but it does not rise above burlesque. Tom is embarrassed by the turn of events, but he is not rebuffed; and Jim's somnolence is not a dignifying substitute for a display of reason and firm conscience. The author's portrayal of Huck in these novels is little better. Both of these later Huck and Tom novels represent a clear falling off, an imaginative failure. Part of the reason for the success of *Huckleberry Finn* resides in Twain's capacity to identify with his heroes, to fully imagine them from within. This quality is obviously lacking in the later novels, where he too often simply puts his characters through their paces without displaying that vivifying sympathy that so invigorated his masterpiece.

Twain's imaginative and ethical attachment to his young hero in *Huckleberry Finn* has been amply explored, but little attention has been given to the basis of identification Twain might have had for Jim. Nor has it been pointed out that the ambitions of this fraternal pair drive against one another: Huck wishes to escape the constraints of civilization and domestication. He initially plans to travel south and tramp about the country. By contrast, Jim hopes to escape into responsibility, society, and civilization—to get a job or "situation," to earn money, and to buy his family out of slavery. He hopes to make it north to Canada. Jim is kept out of the social order except as an item

---

29. *The Adventures of Tom Sawyer, Tom Sawyer Abroad, and Tom Sawyer, Detective,* 315–16.

of property; Huck, on the other hand, is unowned, and personally resistant to the pressures of adoption or the reconstitution of his natural family by returning to live with Pap or of his surrogate family in the Widow Douglas. In Huck, Twain created a character who symbolized a nostalgic return to youth, unencumbered freedom, and mischief; he was a symbol of an imagined past. In Jim's situation there was, perhaps, an analogue to Twain's immediate present.

As Justin Kaplan has observed, Twain was doubly an outsider, one who often explored his internal conflicts and sense of "doubleness" in his fiction.[30] He neither approved of the dominant American culture nor found ready acceptance into it. And he was equally frustrated by both alternatives. He seems to have envied Howells's ability to move so easily among the Boston elite, but both he and Howells overreacted to the failure of Twain's "Whittier Birthday Speech" delivered before such literary worthies as Emerson and Holmes. His embarrassment is the most famous example of his susceptibility to self-condemnation about his behavior in genteel society. Moreover, Twain himself was— and in a very real sense—public property, a man who played so many parts, catered so adroitly to general expectations, that there must have been times when he did not know where his true identity lay. He felt required to be a comic figure and found it difficult to be taken seriously or to speak directly. He had become, in effect, the author of and the actor in his own minstrelsy. In short, his own experience—his sense of personal frustration and moral indignation and social alienation—may have at times seemed parallel to that of the Negro. He may, at times, have felt himself to be a "white nigger." He may have come to despise himself and, like Tom of *Pudd'nhead Wilson,* to have despised the dominant culture that urged such self-hatred upon him. This is rank speculation, of course, but surely there is some significance in the fact that, in 1894, just after he learned of the failure of the Paige typesetting machine and was beset by personal shame, he retreated upstairs and reappeared before his family in blackface.[31]

30. See *Mr. Clemens and Mark Twain,* 100–102.
31. Recorded in Jay Martin's "The Genie in the Bottle: Huckleberry Finn in Mark

Such an attitude would have been supplemented and supported by his developing notions about universal slavery, conditioning and training, notions he would articulate in his essays "What Is Happiness?" and "What Is Man?" and would explore in fictional terms in *Pudd'nhead Wilson* and *A Connecticut Yankee* and that, to a lesser extent, he had already explored in *The Prince and the Pauper*.

Whatever irony Twain intended by Tom's disclosure in the next to the last chapter that Jim is "as free as any cretur that walks this earth" (356) had been effectively rendered by the evasion episode. For in their efforts to "free" Jim, Huck and Tom had resumed those roles that introduced the pair in the opening chapters as naturally as habit itself. And Jim himself had once again become a comic darkie figure. The overruling effects of training and conditioning had been dramatized, but the point had not been sufficiently made. Twain, in the narrative conclusion, suggested a theme of universal slavery, but he may nevertheless have felt compelled to clarify it.

When he wrote the *Walter Scott* episode, he had Jim and Huck attempt to rescue another captive "Jim," Jim Turner. In this episode, Huck wishes Tom were there to guide them in this "adventure" and measures his behavior against Tom Sawyer's code; and the scene does provide a realistic parallel to the romanticized rescue Tom superintends in the evasion chapters. However, the *Walter Scott* episode also qualifies these last chapters because Turner and his criminal captors are to be rescued, but they are not to be "freed." Huck decides to "fix up some kind of yarn, and get somebody to go for that gang and get them out of their scrape, so they can be hung when their time comes" (87). Twain seems also to have recognized that the most appropriate spokesman for his thoughts on universal slavery was one commonly recognized to be a slave, Jim.

At any rate, it is significant that Twain represents this view in *Huckleberry Finn* through Jim rather than any other character when he has him propose that Solomon's mistaken wisdom is the result of his

---

Twain's Life," in Robert Sattelmeyer and J. Donald Crowley, eds., *One Hundred Years of "Huckleberry Finn": The Boy, His Book, and American Culture; Centennial Essays* (Columbia: University of Missouri Press, 1985), 60.

training. Huck insists that Jim misses the point of the Solomon story, and Jim responds:

> Blame de pint! I reck'n I knows what I knows. En mine you, de *real* pint is down furder—it's down deeper. It lays in de way Sollermun was raised. You take a man dat's got on'y one er two chillen: is dat man gwyne to be waseful o' chillen? No, he ain't; he can't 'ford it. *He* know how to value 'em. But you take a man dat's got 'bout five million chillen runnin' roun' de house, en it's diffunt. (96)

Jim speaks with an intellectual conviction that represents Twain's point of view, but Jim's own "make" makes it difficult if not impossible for Twain to argue the point through him, for everything about Jim's training militates against the informed expression of a determinist philosophy. Such philosophizing is a luxury. No one could better understand the terms of slavery than Jim himself, but how is he to express it in any other way than by his own vague, inarticulate yearning for a personal freedom? Besides, "freedom" for Jim means attaining a position within the existing social order, not escaping from its contaminating pressures.

Twain had contemplated in his working notes giving Jim an instant education—he considered having Huck teach him to read and write and does have Huck try to give Jim a history lesson.[32] But he recognized that however profoundly Jim, the slave, might understand the conditions of slavery, Twain, the realist writer, could not have his character comment upon those conditions. More importantly, Jim's behavior throughout the novel repudiated the very convictions he might utter through him. Jim, in exploring the deeper point about Solomon, utters a truth that denies what Twain himself had argued in "What Is Happiness?"—"that the human machine gets all its inspiration from the outside and is not capable of originating an idea of any kind in its own head."[33] And Twain's further observation, in the same essay, that "there is no such thing as self-sacrifice,"

---

32. Twain recorded in Group C of his working notes the following: "Teaches Jim to read & write—then uses dog-messenger. Had taught him a little before." See DeVoto, *Mark Twain at Work*, 75.

33. Quoted in Blair, *Mark Twain and Huck Finn*, 337.

is hardly corroborated by Jim's actions in the novel. Even were one to discount his behavior toward Huck, Jim is so self-sacrificing that he forgoes his chances for freedom and risks lynching when he helps the boy who has caused him so much humiliation and misery, Tom Sawyer.

Jim might have become a carrier of a larger philosophic message than his own debased yet resilient humanity, if indeed there is a larger message. But Twain did not know how to realistically invest his character with the wherewithal to comment upon it. He would try other means to this end in subsequent fictions, but the terms of this novel had been set for some time. In the long run, Jim commanded Twain's sympathy, not his pity, for he had imagined him from within and had projected a portion of himself into the character. Because of this, Jim finally emerges as something more than mere symbol, and more than a mere adjunct to Huck Finn. He is a complex and sympathetic figure, and we as readers are lucky that Twain did not know how to learn him to argue; we are lucky he quit when he did.

THE REALISM OF
HUCKLEBERRY FINN

"Hast seen the White Whale?" gritted Ahab in reply.

"No; only heard of him; but don't believe in him at all," said the other good-humoredly. "Come aboard!"

"Thou are too damned jolly. Sail on. Hast lost any men?"

"Not enough to speak of—two islanders, that's all;—but come aboard."

—*Moby-Dick,* chapter 115, "The Pequod Meets the Bachelor"

"It warn't the grounding—that didn't keep us back but a little. We blowed out a cylinder-head."

"Good gracious! anybody hurt?"

"No'm. Killed a nigger."

"Well, it's lucky; because sometimes people do get hurt."

—*Adventures of Huckleberry Finn,* chapter 32

I

THE SECOND OF THESE passages, too familiar to require much commentary, is frequently instanced as a dramatic rendering of much that is noteworthy about *Huckleberry Finn:* the centrality to the novel's purpose of questions of racial prejudice; the transparent irony disclosed in Aunt Sally's anxious question and her genuine relief that no "people" were injured; the canniness of Huck himself, who, though perplexed by this sudden relative who calls him "Tom," knows enough about human nature to invent yet another fictional experience and to adopt yet another persona on the instant, but who is totally unaware of the satire, irony, or humor of his own remark. Huck knows his audience *inside* the novel; time and again he sizes up his situation in an antagonistic adult world and plays to the several desires, fears, and biases of those who confront or question him. However (despite his amiable introduction to us in the opening paragraph, his final summary complaint about the "trouble" he has had telling his story, and his closing adieu, "YOURS TRULY, HUCK FINN"), Huck is often indifferent to or ignorant of his effects upon an audience *outside* the book, which is to say us as readers.

If realism depends upon a certain consensual understanding of the world, an understanding, that is, of what Henry James said we cannot, one way or another, "not know," then the realism of *Huckleberry Finn* stands in peculiar relation to other realist works. As Michael Davitt Bell has shown, Twain's attachment to the announced principles of literary realism is tenuous at best,[1] and what is true for Twain is even more true for his young narrator. For Huck not only does not knowingly participate in this consensus understanding, but he also is supremely unqualified to render it in his narrative. Time and again, Huck proves that he can readily adapt to the moves of the game, but no one has taught him the logic of it. The origins of feuds, the behavior of pirates and robbers, the decor of the Grangerford house, the prerogatives of royalty, all these remain obscure and mysterious to him, but he quickly sizes up the situation and plays his part as best he can.

The first passage comes from as famous a book. Yet so far as I know this exchange and its coincidentally parallel expression in *Huckleberry Finn* have gone virtually unnoticed. There may be several explanations for this. Among them, and one perhaps worth exploring, involves the difference between the romanticism of *Moby-Dick* and the realism of *Huckleberry Finn*. That difference may be as simple

---

1. "Mark Twain, 'Realism,' and Huckleberry Finn," in *New Essays on "Huckleberry Finn,"* ed. Louis J. Budd (Cambridge: Cambridge University Press, 1985), 35–59.

as the distinction between motive and action, the difference, that is, between quest and escape—between the pursuit (all defiant of necessity and contingency, fixed upon some insane object and driven by some overruling passion) and the "scrape" (the unanticipated event somehow managed, eluded, or negotiated). Ahab bends the will of his crew to his purpose and dispenses with genial observances and courtesies; Huck caters to whim and courts favor, always with an eye to the nearest exit. The unmarried captain of the *Bachelor*, as with most of Melville's bachelors, is an emblem of moral complacency and lavish good humor, in command of a full cargo and homeward bound. Aunt Sally is a type, an equal mixture of Christian goodwill, blind bigotry, and doting affection, glad to receive the boy whom she takes to be her nephew. *Moby-Dick* is characterized by its symbolic trappings, its metaphysical inquiries, its lyrical spontaneity, its Shakespearean "quick probings at the very axis of reality," as Melville said in "Hawthorne and His Mosses."

But *Huckleberry Finn* works by other means: It subverts the same high drama that promotes its episodes (Boggs's drunken swagger, for example, results in his murder, but the dramatic emphasis is upon the town's perverse fascination with his dying; a distempered gang calls for the lynching of Colonel Sherburn, but what they receive is an upbraiding lecture on mob cowardice). It indulges on the happiest terms in reflective moments through the benign auspices of folklore, superstition, and enviable credulity. Ishmael's crow's-nest reverie is blasted by the anxious recognition that he hovers over "Descartesian vortices," but Huck and Jim argue the origins of stars—the moon must have laid them after all—and no one gets hurt. *Huckleberry Finn* displays much less of the Melvillean interest in an "Anacharsis Clootz deputation" of humanity than in the solidarity of two, a "community of misfortune" as Twain would later describe the partnership of Huck and Jim. In the above cited passages, Melville's is a throwaway line, Twain's an epitome of vernacular realism.

Huckleberry Finn, like *Moby-Dick,* is a storyteller's story. In both books the teller and the tale vie for our attention. Ishmael, the yarn-spinner, is intent on chasing to their dens the significances of his experiences, though it is seldom the case that we as readers feel that these adventures are existentially *his* at all. Huck, too, is a receptacle of impressions, but they are filtered through a distinctively adolescent consciousness—quick to perceive, slow to comprehend.

But there are two "authors" of *Huckleberry Finn,* Mark Twain and Huck Finn, and there are also two distinct fictive worlds established by them. Twain presents us with a world that must be judged, Huck with a world that must be inhabited. If both authors are realists, however, their realism is of different orders of experience. Huckleberry Finn's story is primarily a record of feeling, not cognition, and as Twain once remarked, "emotions are among the toughest things in the world to manufacture out of whole cloth; it is easier to manufacture seven facts than one emotion."[2] The "quality of felt life" that Henry James claimed is central to the realist aesthetic is fulfilled in Huck's story; the deadly satirical thrusts of a man slightly outraged by life are largely the result of Twain's management of that same narrative.

The difference between Mark Twain's realism and Huck Finn's may be seen at a glance in comparable passages from *Life on the Mississippi* and *Huckleberry Finn*:

> I had myself called with the four o'clock watch, mornings, for one cannot see too many summer sunrises on the Mississippi. They are enchanting. First, there is the eloquence of silence; for a deep hush broods everywhere. Next, there is the haunting sense of loneliness, isolation, remoteness from the worry and bustle of the world. The dawn creeps in stealthily; the solid walls of black forest soften to gray, and vast stretches of the river open up and reveal themselves; the water is glass-smooth, gives off spectral little wreaths of white mist, there is not the faintest breath of wind, nor stir of leaf; the tranquility is profound and infinitely satisfying. Then a bird pipes up, another follows, and soon the pipings develop into a jubilant riot of music. . . . When the light has become a little stronger, you have one of the fairest and softest pictures imaginable. You have the intense green of the massed and crowded foliage near by; you see it paling shade by shade in front of you; . . . And all this stretch of river is a mirror, and you have the shadowy reflections of the

2. *Life on the Mississippi* (New York: Viking Penguin, 1986), 228–29.

leafage and the curving shores and the receding capes pictured in it. Well, that is all beautiful; soft and rich and beautiful; and when the sun gets well up, and distributes a pink flush here and a powder of gold yonder and a purple haze where it will yield the best effect, you grant that you have seen something that is worth remembering.[3]

In chapter 19, Huck and Jim watch "the daylight come":

Not a sound, anywheres—perfectly still—just like the whole world was asleep, only sometimes the bull-frogs a-cluttering, maybe. The first thing to see, looking away over the water, was a kind of dull line—that was the woods on t'other side—you couldn't make nothing else out; then a pale place in the sky; then more paleness, spreading around; then the river softened up, away off, and warn't black any more, but gray; you could see little dark spots drifting along, ever so far away—trading scows, and such things; and long black streaks—rafts; sometimes you could hear a sweep screaking; or jumbled up voices, it was so still, and sounds come so far; and by and by you could see a streak on the water which you know by the look of the streak that there's a snag there in a swift current which breaks on it and makes that streak look that way; and you see the mist curl up off of the water, and the east reddens up, and the river, and you make out a log cabin in the edge of the woods, away on the bank on t'other side of the river, being a wood-yard, likely, and piled by them cheats so you can throw a dog through it anywheres; then the nice breeze springs up, and comes fanning you from over there, so cool and fresh, and sweet to smell, on account of the woods and the flowers; but sometimes not that way, because they've left dead fish laying around, gars, and such, and they do get pretty rank; and next you've got the full day, and everything smiling in the sun, and the song-birds just going it! (156–57)

Disclosed here are the obvious differences to be expected between a genteel and a vernacular narrator, or more properly between an adult and a child. Twain's passage is deliberate—shaped by rhetorical motive, organized logically in homogenous time and space, varied in diction, consistent in tone, and obedient to the terms of its

3. Ibid.

announced purpose. Descriptive detail corroborates the preordained sentiment; the hushed silence, the creeping mists, the massed color and softening light contribute to, even validate, the "enchantment" of the scene.

Huck's description moves by statement and correction—there is "not a sound," he says, "but only sometimes"; the air is "sweet to smell" but "sometimes" there is a dead gar laying around. There is in Huck's passage the unembarrassed monotony of phrasing—the word *streak* is used three times in the same clause. And Huck dispenses with explanatory remark. Twain's river is a mirror in which are to be found the reflections of wood and shore, but when Huck says "and the east reddens up, and the river" there is no authorial indication that the river reflects the red of the sky, for his world need not answer to the laws of optics. The phenomenon is local to his perception; it would not occur to him that the scene is an "effect." Huck's river at dawn is shifting impressions first and only incidentally a world of objects—the "little dark spots," we are told by way of an appositive, are trading scows; the "dull line," the woods; the "long black streaks," rafts. His world is populated by things, but they don't authorize his experience. And he does not belabor the mental corrections necessary to make such a world.

Twain's description is a "composition," a self-conscious act of language so constructed that we may grant that the scene is "worth remembering." Whether or not his depiction is memorably phrased, it stands as admiration of a natural event whose picturesque existence is independent of his rendering. Huck's scene is merely recalled, and one feels that without his consciousness to sustain it, the world itself might dissolve. For all that, however, Huck's landscape is the more tolerant; it admits the coexistence of the duplicity of cheats and stench of rotting fish with the music of birds. Huck is ever alert to treachery and snare, yet without condemning, he delivers an undiminished natural scene and exults in a privileged moment. Twain, by contrast, aims at a universal sentiment that is tonic relief from the "worry and bustle of the world."

Twain's presence pervades *Huckleberry Finn,* but with few exceptions, he is loyal to the terms of the book and favors Huck's unmediated world of feeling over his own often angry conviction.[4] That is, however strong Twain's own sentiments, he typically recognized that his first artistic responsibility was to a rendering of the authenticity of Huck's adolescent sensibility. The realism of *Huckleberry Finn* is disclosed alternately by the thread of Huck's consciousness, not yet come to full awareness of how fully implicated in events it is, and by the palpable events that seem randomly strung upon it, which is to say by the narrative itself. These are inevitably interwoven, and often tangled, but it is well to take up the teller and the tale separately.

II

One of the things to be observed about the realism of *Huckleberry Finn* is that Huck's voice functions much like Whitman's multivalent "I" in "Song of Myself"—he is the narrator of his chronicle and the author of his book; he is the chief witness of events and, emotionally at least, the principal victim of them; he is ruled and to a degree protected by the laws of the republic and the customs of place, but only accidentally a citizen of and never a voice in the dominant culture that so mystifies him.

Both as "author" and as narrator, Huck typically forgoes representational depiction. He himself has seen the Aunt Sallys of the world before, and he is far less interested in disclosing her character than in dealing with the situation. Huck's own considerable experience in the world (the result of having fended for himself most times, not of playing the detached observer of life), as remarkable as it is regrettable in a fourteen-year-old child, outfits him for his adventures. In this sense, the realism of the quoted passage above, and dozens of others like it, is presupposed in the telling itself.[5] Unlike

4. Twain does speak his own mind from time to time—most obviously when he has Colonel Sherburn scold the mob in chapter 22, and perhaps most interestingly when he chooses to speak through Jim about the benefits of industry and progress in parts of chapter 14.

5. Shaped as he is by experience, however, Huck remains innocent in an impor-

Ahab, Huck takes the world on its terms, not his own, and experience has taught him how to best navigate its treacheries and to delight in its beauties.

Huck's wary canniness is frequently the source in *Huckleberry Finn* of the sort of narrative detachment so often associated with realist writing; it is also the source of a special pathos. When Huck sees the king and the duke tarred and feathered, men who "didn't look like nothing in the world that was human," he is incapable of hardening himself to their plight. Huck finally concludes, "Human beings *can* be awful cruel to one another" (290). This familiar scene is moving not because it effectively dramatizes Twain's attitudes toward the damned human race, nor for that matter because it serves as moral pronouncement (these two con men are scalawags through and through and deserve the sort of treatment they at long last receive). Nor, I believe, does it signal Huck's moral development, or as Leo Marx would have it, "a mature blending of his instinctive suspicion of human motives with his capacity for pity."[6] Instead, it is the unlooked for and disquieting revelation, somewhat surprising in a boy as familiar with the world as Huck is, that gives the moment force.

For Huck has witnessed earlier far greater and more disturbing cruelty than this: the murderous treatment of Jim Turner on the *Walter Scott;* the killing of Buck Grangerford, which still troubles his sleep; Boggs's gasping out his last breath under the weight of a family Bible; not to mention the thievery and calculated deceptions of the king and the duke themselves. What he hasn't before recognized, indeed does not fully recognize even as he speaks his sad

---

tant way. Unlike Colonel Sherburn, say, who has traveled in the North and lived in the South and is therefore able to proclaim on the cowardice of the "average" man (190), Huck's perspective has not frozen into an attitude. Not only is the narrative point of view of this novel presexual, as has so often been observed, but it is also prepolitical, even preideological. Huck, in his efforts to help Jim, may worry that he may become a "low-down Abolitionist," but the quality of that anxiety is rather more like a thousand childhood myths—e.g., the worry children have that, having made an ugly face, it will "stick."

6. "Mr. Eliot, Mr. Trilling, and Huckleberry Finn," *The American Scholar* 22 (Autumn 1953): 423–40.

conclusion, is the universal human condition of cruelty. Nor has he yet developed the righteous, which is to say the "civilized," indignation that would serve as defense against his own spontaneous impulses.

Huck and Tom have no opportunity to help these con men, and they go on home. But Huck is feeling "kind of ornery and humble," not so brash as before, even though he knows he hasn't done anything to cause the event he has just witnessed. Only two chapters earlier, in his famous decision to tear up the letter to Miss Watson and to "go to hell" and to help Jim, Huck's sympathies had prevailed against his training. Twain once observed in reference to a similar internal struggle in chapter 16, that this is a chapter "where a sound heart and a deformed conscience come into collision and conscience suffers defeat." His analogous moral decision in chapter 31 is a temporary triumph, however; as Harold H. Kolb, Jr., has remarked, "Huck never defeats his deformed conscience—it is we [as readers] who do that—he simply ignores it in relation to Jim."[7] When he sees the punished king and duke, however, Huck finds that a conscience, deformed or otherwise, has little to do with whether you do right or wrong or nothing at all. And precisely at that moment conscience moves in on him: "If I had a yaller dog that didn't know no more than a person's conscience, I would pison him. It takes up more room than all the rest of a person's insides, and yet ain't no good, nohow" (290).

Perhaps Huck is never so vulnerable as at this moment. His unwanted recognition, followed hard and fast by voracious conscience, has its inverted equivalent in *Moby-Dick* when Ahab realizes his quest is self-destructive but that he must press on nevertheless, and he drops his tear into the sea. For in Huck's response to the frenzied throng of townspeople exacting their revenge on these rapscallions and the image of the pair who do not look human, he concludes upon the human condition. Ahab is driven by interior impulses that

---

7. Twain, quoted in Walter Blair, *Mark Twain and Huck Finn* (Berkeley and Los Angeles: University of California Press, 1960), 143; Kolb, "Mark Twain, Huck Finn, and Jacob Blivens: Gilt-Edged, Tree-Calf Morality in the *Adventures of Huckleberry Finn*," *The Virginia Quarterly Review* 55 (Autumn 1979): 658.

extinguish all "natural" longings and lovings; but Huck, just as relentlessly, and simply by virtue of being alive and growing up, is being drawn into this inhuman, human world.

Robinson Jeffers, in "Shine, Perishing Republic," would have his children keep their distance from the "thickening center" of corruption:

And boys, be in nothing so moderate as in love of man, a clever servant,
    insufferable master.
There is the trap that catches noblest spirits, that caught—they say—
    God, when he walked the earth.

This is a belated wisdom, reduced to fatherly advice, that, boys being boys, will likely go all unheeded. But Twain (or Huck rather) dramatizes his troubled understanding at the moment of its birth; his conclusion is the unstudied remark, not yet a conviction, no longer a perception. For Huck, corruption has no center but spreads out evenly before him, just as he has left it behind in the wake of his flight; it presents no scrape to be mastered or outlived but the general human condition. And Huck is not yet wise; his insight yields instantly to vague, unaccountable feelings of guilt. And this, too, is a dimension of the realism of the book, for he is a boy more ruled by feeling than sober reflection.

Huckleberry Finn has sometimes been described as a picaresque novel without the picaro. This may be a meaningful statement if our understanding of the genre is qualified by the variations of it Cervantes accomplished in *Don Quixote,* a novel Twain read several times, Tom Sawyer at least once, and Huck not at all. Still, Huck is not quite an idealist, not yet a rogue. His mischievousness is typical of a boy his age, and it is combined with a special, sometimes ridiculous tenderness.

Huck is often capable of pseudomoralizing, citing his Pap as authority for lifting a chicken or borrowing a melon. This is also true when, in chapter 22, he dodges the watchman and dives under the circus tent: "I had my twenty-dollar gold piece and some other money, but I reckoned I better save it. . . . I ain't opposed to spending money on circuses, when there ain't no other way, but there ain't no use in *wasting* it on them" (191). Once inside, though the audience is hilarious, Huck is "all of a tremble" to see the danger of the drunken horseback rider. When, at length, he recognizes that he has been taken in by this performer, he is so admiring of him and the bully circus itself that he claims if he ever runs across it again, "it can have all of *my* custom, every time" (194).

In this relatively slight episode are compactly blended the multiple functions of Huck as author, character, narrator, and comic device. As author, he tries to make the circus scene vivid to us, but he is not equal to the task. His rendering of the performance is notable for its descriptive flatness. The passages are sprinkled with a few vernacular metaphors, but unlike his disturbing description of his Pap in chapter 5, Huck's language here is indefinite and vague. The men are dressed in their "drawers and under-shirts," he says, and the ladies have lovely complexions and are "perfectly beautiful." What *is* vivid, however, is his faltering speech, his slightly breathless excitement. As narrator, he gropes for adjectives and falls into abstractions and platitudes. Huck is mastered by the spectacle, which is simultaneously his experience and his subject matter. But as boy, he is true to childlike enthusiasm and typically replaces descriptive detail with hyperbolic affidavits of his rapt attention: it was "the splendidest sight that ever was"; the women looked like "real sure-enough queens"; it was a "powerful fine sight"; "I never see anything so lovely"; "they done the most astonishing things" (191–92). At length, he becomes the straight man to his own joke. So pleased is he with the sight that he promises the circus can have his business any time, evidently unaware of the humor of the remark, that his "custom" has in no way damaged his purse.

Huck is worldly wise but never jaded, as this episode dramatizes, but the significance of his pranks are defined less by youthful motive than by the terms of the adventure. The charm of what Neil Schmitz calls his "Huckspeech" (speech "written as spoken, talked into prose")[8] can be, and is, radically redefined by narrative context. There is

8. *of Huck and Alice: Humorous Writing in American Literature* (Minneapolis: University of Minnesota Press, 1983), 96.

prankishness involved, for example, when Huck plays his joke on Jim after they have been separated in the fog, but he receives a tongue-lashing that so cuts him that he "humbles himself to a nigger." Huck's manufacture of his own murder in order to escape the potentially lethal abuse of his Pap is grotesque to be sure, but it is highly dramatic too, and Huck regrets that Tom is not handy to throw in "the fancy touches" (41). He laments Tom's absence as well in an episode that is a mixture of romantic escapade and existential urgency when, in chapter 12, he and Jim undertake to save Jim Turner from certain death. The same may be said for his efforts to preserve the Wilks girls' fortune from the hands of the king and the duke.

As humorist Huck is humorless, as hero he is only accidentally heroic, and as narrator he seems never quite to know where to place the accent. He is constitutionally incapable of distilling from his supposed experience either the ultimate conditions or the deeper significance of his adventures. Huck never doubts the existence of the "bad place" and the "good place"; in fact, he believes them to be all that Miss Watson has told him. However, while he can imagine the fires of hell and the monotony of playing harps and singing forever, he scarcely comprehends eternity and has little interest in it. His famous declaration "All right, then, I'll *go* to hell" (271) is not accompanied with an exclamation point. The statement is matter-of-fact and to be taken literally, for Huck is a literal-minded boy. He is temperamentally suited to the bad place (wickedness is in his line, he says), and he will give up trying to achieve the other place. But his decision is also the resignation of self-acceptance, a declaration, that is, of the acceptance of the world's judgment upon him, not the resolution to abide by some higher moral authority, as is sometimes claimed. It is just this quality that gives the scene its special pathos. Huck is not built right, and the fact that he is social and moral refuse is hardly arguable.

Huck is caught between stern rebuke ("Don't scrunch up like that, Huckleberry"; "Don't gap and stretch like that") and enforced social acceptance ("Pray every day, Huckleberry"; "Chew your food, Huckleberry"). But he remains the same boy the town allowed to sleep in a hogshead, stay away from school, and make do for himself. Caught on the horns of this dilemma, there is nevertheless a strong undercurrent of self-affirmation; Huck is filled with self-recrimination and self-condemnation, but never self-loathing. When Jim is bitten by the rattlesnake, he curses himself as a "fool" for not remembering that the mate was apt to join the dead one he had placed in Jim's blanket; he is sorry for the outcome and his stupidity but not the impulse. Huck devoutly tries to admire Emmeline's poetic "tributes" and drawings because he accepts the Grangerford family faith that she was a saint; he even steals up into her room and browses through her scrapbook when he begins to "sour" on her. He often regrets that Tom Sawyer is not around to throw some style into his plans, but Huck never fully accepts the world's corrections or refusals of him. And this same realistic disclosure of a young boy's self-consciousness, in the hands of Mark Twain, becomes a satirical vehicle as well.

Twain often employs a satirical strategy in Huck that he seems to have observed in himself and to have dramatized in *A Tramp Abroad*. The narrator of that book does not condemn violent alien customs (most particularly the revolting German student duels) but instead curses himself for failing to comprehend the wisdom of received tradition. The same is true of countless occasions in *Huckleberry Finn* where Twain's intent, as opposed to Huck's, is to expose sham, pretense, and outright silliness: Huck is perplexed that the widow makes him "grumble over the victuals" even though there is nothing wrong with them; he takes it on faith that Emmeline Grangerford's pictures are "nice," but they always give him the "fan-tods"; he goes to church with the Grangerfords and hears a sermon about brotherly love and "preforeordestination," and everyone agrees it was a good sermon, and it must be so because, for Huck, it proved to be "one of the roughest Sundays" he had ever run across.

Tom Sawyer variously describes Huck as a lunkhead, an idiot, or a saphead for failing to comprehend the observances required of pirates, robbers, or royalty. Huck never disputes Tom's basic superiority or his own cultural and moral ignorance; after all, Tom is "full of principle" (307). In fact, Huck is flabbergasted that Tom is willing and eager to help him free Jim, and he regrets his own betrayal of his friend for not insisting that he not sink so low:

> Here was a boy that was respectable, and well brung up; and had a character to lose; and folks at home that had characters; and he was bright and not leatherheaded; and knowing, and not ignorant; and not mean, but kind; and yet here he was, without any more pride, or rightness, or feeling, than to stoop to this business, and make himself a shame, and his family a shame, before everybody. I *couldn't* understand it, no way at all. (292–93)

As a realistic portrayal of one boy's concern for another, the statement is touching; as satire, it is deadly—all the more so when we learn that Miss Watson has already freed Jim in her will and that Tom knows it.

Twain once astutely remarked that, unlike *Tom Sawyer, Huckleberry Finn* is not a book for boys but for those who used to be boys. It is not altogether clear Twain recognized this distinction at the time of writing the novel, so strong was his identification with his created character, but the instinctive decision to have an unwashed fourteen-year-old outcast tell a story ultimately meant for readers whose own innocence was behind them proved to be an enabling one. As a character or narrative consciousness, Huck is pure possibility—his future casually spreads out before him, luxuriant in meandering adventures and antics, freedom and easiness. But he is doomed as well—for every adult reader knows (though because we are adults we are often reluctant to admit it) that his delightful caginess and high jinks depend less on moral purpose than on youthful energy; his escapes and accommodations are destined to become evasions and compromises in the end.[9] Huck does not know this, he hasn't even considered the issue; but we his grown-up readers do, and every vile specimen of humanity surveyed in this rich cross section of America confirms it. Huckleberry Finn set out to tell a story and did the best he could. By degrees, it became apparent to Mark Twain that the boy was writing a novel.

9. Twain knew this, too; in a cranky moment, he predicted that Huck would grow up to be just as low-down and mean as his Pap.

III

Perhaps *novel* is too narrow a word. In his "Notice," and apparently after some deliberation, Twain chose to describe his book as a "narrative." In any event, the tale Huck tells is all slapdash and Oh, by the way, as mixed up in its way as the king's recitation of Hamlet's soliloquy; the book Twain wrote is another matter.

Huckleberry Finn is a highly episodic book, and the arrangement of episodes observes no incontestable narrative logic. The feud chapters precede rather than follow the Boggs shooting not for self-evident artistic reasons but because we are to suppose that is the order in which Huck lived them. The episodic density of the book thins considerably as the narrative progresses, the last half being dominated by the lost heirs episode and the evasion chapters. But this is not because these events are more important than earlier ones but because in the several-year gestation of the book Twain himself had acquired the capacity to make more of less. That capacity, it is true, sometimes degenerates into artifice and burlesque, as in the strategy to acquire one of Aunt Sally's spoons, but it likewise betrays an author's professionally calculated attitude toward his material. Moreover, Twain had commercial as well as artistic motives impelling him to finish his book; undoubtedly, in the final burst of composition in 1883, he approached his narrative, in part, as a commodity that was too long in production. Besides, he had his own newly formed publishing company ready to print and promote it.

The *reason* some episodes follow others might be more confidently pursued by examining how the novel grew and took shape during the seven years of its intermittent composing. That is a story too complicated to tell here.[10] It is enough to say, perhaps, that Huck Finn, as character and voice, was a metaphor for Twain's mind: through his identification with the boy he might indulge nostalgically in vagrant thoughts and happy recollections, and particularly in

---

10. Walter Blair and, more recently, Victor A. Doyno have provided us with full and perceptive book-length studies of the evolution of the novel. See Blair, *Mark Twain and Huck Finn,* and Doyno, *Writing Huck Finn: Mark Twain's Creative Process* (Philadelphia: University of Pennsylvania Press, 1991).

the early stages of composition he might satisfy his own desire to escape the cares of a world that was too much with him. And when he was in more aggressive moods, through the satirical latitude Huck's perspective on events permitted him, Twain could deal scathingly with his several hatreds and annoyances—racial bigotry, mob violence, self-righteousness, aristocratic pretense, venality and duplicity, along with several lesser evils. His complaints about these and other matters found their way into Huck's narrative.

W. D. Howells once affectionately complained that he wished Mark Twain might rule his fancy better, and for his part, Twain contributed to the public image of him as a jackleg novelist. However, not since the work of such critics as Gladys Bellamy, Sydney Krause, William Gibson, Walter Blair, Victor Doyno, or Henry Nash Smith, to name only a few, has anyone been able to celebrate Twain's maverick genius at the expense of his literary art. Still, we cannot dismiss out of hand Mark Twain's claim that he merely served as the "amanuensis" to his creative imagination, and in fact on the first page of the manuscript of the novel he gave his book the working title "Huckleberry Finn/Reported by Mark Twain." By the end of the first paragraph, however, even that modest claim seems too much.

From the manuscript we know that Twain had at first begun his tale with "You will not know about me . . ." before he fully accepted Huck's ungrammatical authenticity and, with it, all the multiplying implications of the decision. "You don't know about me," Huck begins, "without you have read a book by the name of 'The Adventures of Tom Sawyer.'" Clearly, Mark Twain cannot serve even as the reporter of Huck's narrative, and, besides, he is not to be trusted, for we have it on Huck's authority that he told some "stretchers" in recounting Tom's story. Within the first three sentences, Huck has politely dispensed with "Mr. Mark Twain" and introduced himself as an orphan in more ways than one.

Except perhaps for the opening lines of "Song of Myself," there may be no more audacious beginning to an extended work of the imagination. Mysteriously, we are forced, or rather agree, to assume what Huck assumes, not because we are in the seductive presence of someone afoot with his vision, but because Huck amuses us. He makes us laugh and, later, cry; we want to be with him and to hear him speak. Just as mysteriously, we assume, or rather never ask, how such a book written by a boy could come to be, nor do we require of it even the most fundamental elements of fictional probability.

Even without Kemble's illustration of Huck writing a letter to Mary Jane Wilks in chapter 28, we can easily imagine him in the act of writing itself—squinting one eye, holding his tongue between his teeth, tightly clenching his pencil as he begins to record his adventures. It is somewhat more difficult, however, to imagine when or why Huck tells his story. We know that he has finished it before he lights out for the Territory and that he has presumably spent about as much time writing as it took for Tom's bullet wound to heal. But the only apparent motive he has in the writing is to correct the forgivably exaggerated account of Tom and him that Mark Twain had published as "The Adventures of Tom Sawyer." (It would be out of character for Huck to assume that anyone might actually be interested in his thoughts or exploits.) More perplexing is the fact that *Tom Sawyer* was published in 1876, but the novel takes place in the 1830s or 1840s, and it never occurs to Huck that he ought to explain this curious discrepancy. It is equally unimaginable that Huck should have lit out for New York instead of the Indian Territory to seek a publisher for the completed manuscript. The very conditions of the fiction that is his book are perhaps the biggest stretcher of all.

It is not for nothing that Twain added the elaborate introductory apparatus to his novel—the heliotype image of him as a frontispiece, sternly presiding over his book; his parenthetical identification of Huck as "Tom Sawyer's Comrade"; his setting of the scene and the time of the novel; his "Notice" and his "Explanatory." These were no doubt, in part, attempts to reassert his own authorial presence in the narrative to follow, but Twain has also rather generously and succinctly made up for some of Huck's literary failings. Huck, after all, never tells us the when or where of this narrative, but Twain does—the Mississippi Valley, forty to fifty years ago. Perhaps Huck did not know, after all, that his story ought to display some interest in motive, plot, or moral, and Twain in his "Notice" somewhat protectively and very authoritatively warns us away from even noting their absence in the narrative. At the same time, in his "Explanatory," Twain calls attention to one of the book's chief virtues, the careful attention to and realistic rendering of dialect. We can imagine Huck straining to parse out a sentence, but we hardly expect him to have taken the same pains Twain did in fashioning the speech of his characters.

Huck's story as novel is impossibility followed by implausibility and linked together by unlikelihood. To give a merely incidental example, when in chapter 17 Huck wakes up after his first night at the Grangerford house, he has forgotten that he is now George Jackson. That much is realistic; the reader, too, is apt to get lost in the dizzying array of Huck's aliases. But Huck tricks Buck into giving the name away:

> "Can you spell, Buck?"
> "Yes," he says.
> "I bet you can't spell my name," says I.
> "I bet you what you dare I can," says he.
> "All right," says I, "go ahead."
> "G-o-r-g-e J-a-x-o-n—there now," he says. (136)

Then Huck privately writes the name down because "somebody might want *me* to spell it, next." One need not be a metafictionist to see the difficulty here. Huck, as narrator, has spelled George Jackson correctly from the beginning, along with any number of other, more difficult names—Harney Shepherdson, Emmeline Grangerford, Lafe Buckner, Silas Phelps, "Henry the Eight," Colonel Sherburn (how Huck was able to sound out *Colonel* is a permanent puzzle). Are we to suppose that in the few months since this exchange with Buck occurred that Huck has undergone some orthographically redemptive experience? My point here is not to indulge in fastidious fault-finding but rather to note that in the course of reading these sorts of questions simply don't come up. The enchantment, the atmosphere of mind, conveyed by Huck's narrative presence is too pleasing, too hypnotic, to permit skepticism. There is considerable magic in the realism of *Huckleberry Finn*.

However improvised and shapeless the boy's narrative is, it nonetheless miraculously coheres almost in spite of itself. More often than not, the plot thickens only to dissolve into another overlapping adventure. We expect Colonel Sherburn to get lynched; but he does not. What really happened to Buck Grangerford; Huck won't tell us. We become interested in the romance of Miss Sophia and Harney Shepherdson, but all we know of their star-crossed love affair is that they got across the river safely. We pity Boggs's sixteen-year-old daughter and ask for revenge; but what we get in her potential hero, Buck Harkness, is a coward and someone looking "tolerable cheap" at that. We hope that the king and duke get their just deserts, but then are made to feel sorry for them when they do. We wish to see the Wilks girls reunited with their money and their nearest kin, but in the climactic scene of this episode the crowd rushes forward to the coffin and Huck takes the opportunity amid the confusion to get away from there, and we, his readers, however much a part of us might want to linger, are willingly drawn after him. The Wilks girls' adventure is abruptly over, and Huck's has acquired new life.

And the two principal plot devices, it turns out, are false leads, Hitchcockean MaGuffins: Huck is fleeing from Pap, but Pap, we learn at last, was the dead man in the floating house thirty-four chapters and several hundred miles ago. Jim is escaping from the dreadful edict of Miss Watson to sell him down the river, but, again, we eventually discover that he had been freed two months earlier in her will. Time and again, the action that enlists our interest is discarded, diverted, or thwarted. In "Chapter the Last" Twain, through several disclosures made by several characters, goes about tying up the loose ends of the story as quickly and efficiently as a calf-roper with the rope clenched between his teeth: Jim owns himself, and his early prophecy that he will be a rich man is fulfilled; Pap is dead, and thus Huck has free use of his six thousand dollars to finance a trip west; Tom is recovered from his bullet wound, and we now know why he had consented to free Jim.

If there is no plot to speak of, there remain nevertheless discernible mythic, structural, and satirical patterns throughout the novel— patterns of flight and absorption, prophecy and fulfillment, retreat and return, death and rebirth, initiation and emergence, repetition and variation. And there are multiple themes and issues as well—of the comic and devastating effects of Christian piety and absurd sentimentality, of obnoxious aristocratic privilege and backwater vulgarity, of marginalization and co-optation, of intuitive sympathy and utilitarian conduct, of inflexible racist bigotry and the dignifying enlargements of open friendship. Then there is the clear advance over and inestimable contribution to the tradition of American humor that is accomplished in the example of the book itself. These patterns, themes, and achievements are certainly "there" within the novel to the extent that criticism and interpretation can make them so, but they would be invisible to Huck and likely hazy to Twain himself. All of them may be comprehended, perhaps, in the insightful remark of Henry Nash Smith: Twain's "technical accomplishment was of course inseparable from the process of discovering new meanings in his material. His development as a writer was a dialectic interplay in which the reach of his imagination imposed a constant strain on his technical resources, and innovations of method in turn opened up new vistas before his imagination."[11]

The four groups of working notes for the novel Twain jotted down between 1879 and 1883 nevertheless reveal that Twain's imaginative reach was at times blind groping. Among other things, Twain considered including in his narrative a Negro sermon, the legend of a Missouri earthquake, a house-raising, a village fire, a hazing, elocution lessons, an encounter with alligators, a quilting bee, a candy-pulling, a temperance lecture, a duel, a lynching, an accidental killing with an "unloaded" gun, an auction, a dog messenger, and (most improbably of all) an elephant given to Huck and Tom so that they might ride around the country and "make no end of trouble."[12] Twain was always tempted by burlesque, of course, and the fact that he resisted the several temptations suggested by this list of creative brainstorms testifies to more than a bit of artistic restraint. However, many have felt he so yielded to his fondness for burlesque in the final evasion episode that he irreparably damaged Huck's integrity

11. *Mark Twain: The Development of a Writer* (Cambridge: Harvard University Press, 1962), 113.

12. The working notes for *Huckleberry Finn* are reproduced in the California-Iowa edition of the novel, 711–61.

and credibility, subjected Jim to a series of unnecessary degradations, subverted the terms of Huck and Jim's friendship he had so patiently developed, and ultimately betrayed his reader's confidence.

That is an issue individual readers will decide, but the working notes indicate at least the range of possibilities Huck's adventures suggested to the author, a range so vast as to become arbitrary. The only requirements of his then developing narrative, it seems, were that Huck should have been the witness to the events, or to a recitation of them by another, and that Huck narrate them. This is merely to say that Twain banked on the realism of a literary manner over and above the realism of subject matter. Any and all of the events recorded in his working notes conceivably could have happened along the Mississippi, of course, but they indicate no definite narrative direction. And many episodes he did dramatize are no less adventitious than those he contemplated. After all, he did choose to include witch pies and rope ladders, hidden treasure and secret tattoos, sideshows and soliloquies, feuds and romances, ghost stories and fistfights. And as palpable as the river is in the book, it is absolutely incredible that a runaway slave should be trying to get to Canada on its current.

If Twain did not in every instance manage to rule his fancy, he does seem to have tried to coordinate the several products of it. The most obvious example of this sort of artistic management is in the telling juxtaposition of the Boggs shooting with the drunken bareback rider at the circus. In the first episode, the actual physical suffering of Boggs and the emotional grief of his daughter are mixed with the sham of pious sentiment and the predictably perverse fascination of the townspeople, who shove each other aside to get a good look at a dying man. At the circus, Huck's worrying over the supposed drunk is sincere, but the man's peril is merely show business. There are other paired episodes or details as well: the actual deafness of Jim's daughter and the deaf-and-dumb hoax of the duke; the real rattlesnake on Jackson's Island that bites Jim and the garter snakes with buttons tied to their tails in the shed at the Phelps farm; Huck's captivity in his Pap's cabin and the gruesomely imagined evidence of his invented murder, and Jim's captivity in the shed on

the Phelps farm and the ridiculous traces of Tom's romantic prescrip-
tions that convince the townsfolk that Jim is a raving lunatic; Huck's
efficient attempts to save Jim Turner aboard the *Walter Scott* and
Tom's embroidered and leisurely efforts to rescue Jim in the evasion
episode. Each of these correspondences, and others as well, mark
with deadly satirical effect the difference between realistic urgency
and contrived hoax. They also mark how artfully Twain blended the
two.

Many of the characters and episodes in *Huckleberry Finn* can be
explained as inspired narrative twists that keep the plot moving
along, broaden the range of Huck and Jim's adventures, and permit
the author to indulge in such imaginative improvisation as might
occur to him. The most important of these are the introduction of
the king and duke in chapter 19 and the reemergence of Tom Sawyer
in chapter 33. When Twain allowed the king and duke to comman-
deer the raft, he violated the sanctity of the craft and the river itself.
But it was also an enabling move, for now his characters could travel
in daylight and the author could survey in freer fashion the manners
and language of life along the river. The maneuver also helped explain away the difficulty of moving an escaped slave into the Deep
South, since Huck and Jim now have considerably less say in events.
The fantastic reintroduction of Tom Sawyer, who suddenly becomes
the superintendent of affairs and relaxes the deadly serious consequences of Huck's decision in chapter 31 to help Jim, turned Huck's
experiences and commitment into disappointingly fanciful pranks.
But at least it provided a strategy, however improbable, for concluding a book that might have drifted along forever.

Huckleberry Finn was published in England in 1884; coincidentally,
Henry James published his famous essay "The Art of Fiction" the
same year. Twain's novel passes most of the tests for the art of the
novel that James proposes there—that it be interesting, that it represent life and give the very "atmosphere of mind" in contact with
experience, that it "catch the color, the relief, the expression, the
surface, the substance of the human spectacle." It also happens to
fulfill the requirements of some critics and the expectations of many
readers that James holds up for skeptical scrutiny—that it have a

"happy ending," that it be full of incident and movement, that it have an obvious moral purpose. Coincidentally, too, James compares in the same essay two novels he had at the time been reading—Robert Louis Stevenson's *Treasure Island* and Edmond de Goncourt's *Chérie*. The first, he notes, "treats of murders, mysteries, islands of dreadful renown, hairbreadth escapes, miraculous coincidences, and buried doubloons"; the second seeks to trace "the development of the moral consciousness of a child." James approves of Stevenson's novel because it achieves what it attempts, whereas De Goncourt's, in his estimation, does not. James probably did not imagine, even as he struck the comparison, that any writer, much less an American writer, might effectively fuse both attempts in a single project, but he certainly would have approved the attempt.

Not that Twain would have given a fig for James's approval. In such matters, W. D. Howells was Twain's admired comrade, as Hawthorne was Melville's. Even so, after Twain had finished his novel and was making revisions, he wrote Howells with a certain petulant self-confidence that he, at least, was happy with the result: "And *I* shall *like* it, whether anybody else does or not." Melville's summary remark to Hawthorne upon the achievement of *Moby-Dick,* to risk one final comparison, is similarly defiant: "I have written a wicked book, and feel spotless as a lamb." The wickedness of *Huckleberry Finn* is not the wickedness of *Moby-Dick,* of course, but it is the sort one might expect of Huck Finn, and maybe Mark Twain. For Huck had been brought up to it, and the rendering of it was right in Twain's line.

HUCKLEBERRY FINN'S HEIRS

I

WHEN ONE TAKES UP the question of the legacy of Mark Twain and more particularly that of *Huckleberry Finn,* one takes up a question of American literary and cultural history. As Louis J. Budd has so compellingly shown, "Mark Twain" is a cultural property in whom Samuel Clemens invested much of his creative energy, an image whose manufacture and marketing he carefully monitored. That image has since gone the way of most slickly advertised commodities and has lost much of its aggressive force; if its fire has dimmed, however, its glow remains perhaps too comfortably available to us.[1] Despite the legion of Twain scholars devoted to amassing, interpreting, and consolidating the ever growing store of information about Twain and his work, one senses that he has become a self-perpetuating institution whose interest and vitality depend very little upon scholarly or critical opinion. Even if the American public were suddenly to become as ignorant and illiterate as so many of his fictional creations it has one way or another come to know and embrace, even if a multitude of scholars and critics were to close the

1. *Our Mark Twain: The Making of His Public Personality,* (Philadelphia: University of Pennsylvania Press, 1983). In our own time, Budd writes, Mark Twain's public personality "stands in danger of functioning as Everybody's Mark Twain in a much less fundamental or provocative way than during his prime" (230). In part, this essay means to explore and speculate about the loss of power of Mark Twain as a literary benefactor rather than as a public commodity. Still, these two elements of Twain's legacy are inevitably intertwined.

shop and go fishing, even if politicians were to cease quoting and misquoting him, the living legacy that is "Mark Twain" (by no means the least interesting of Clemens's imaginative creations) would continue to function in its haphazard but persistent and palpable way.

This is an inquiry into a literary bequest, and I shall at length explore the relations three writers in particular (Ring Lardner, Willa Cather, and Langston Hughes) bear to Twain and especially to the achievement of *Huckleberry Finn*. The examples of these three do not begin to indicate the possibilities or the existing realities of an imaginative inheritance, nor are they the most obvious choices one ought to make if the concern is with being convincing rather than suggestive. But, together, these very different writers do exemplify both the variable richness and, at least in the case of Lardner, the particular burdens of the patrimony of Huckleberry Finn. These same literary relations are separable from the institution that has become "Mark Twain," of course, but the full extent of Twain's literary influence or the larger significance of his place within our culture cannot be fully comprehended without first acknowledging, even in a superficial way, how completely he has entered and helped to define the popular American point of view. For, unlike other American authors, it is simply not the case that Mark Twain is merely an academic specialty. Like it or not, Twain criticism must take into account and to a degree respond to popular reception and understanding. Whether the general public has "got Twain right" is finally beside the point. Because Mark Twain is an American institution, the public will always have a say in how he is to be understood. Scholars or critics who remain indifferent to popular belief about the man or his work will have missed much that is significant in their subject. And if their methods or vocabulary are persistently arcane or obscure, the response of the common reader, sooner or later, will serve as tonic corrective to the indulgence.

Mark Twain is "ours" by virtue of a participation in a social community that forges and forever modifies a consensual view of all its institutions. Mark Twain and Huck Finn are not to be found in archives and libraries alone. I have myself cashed a check at the Mark Twain Bank. I have visited the Tom Sawyer Youth League, on whose field Huck Finn Little League teams sometimes play. I have traveled through the Mark Twain Forest and, in another state, driven on the Clemens Center Parkway. I have passed a real estate company called Mark Twain Properties, and Mark Twain Country Antiques, Mark Twain Travel Agency, Mark Twain Motor Inn, and the Huck Finn Motel. I have declined the opportunity to have a Becky Thatcher burger, but I have played eighteen holes on the Mark Twain Community Golf Course and know firsthand why Twain thought golf "is a good walk spoiled."

All this is by way of saying that the literary portion of Twain's bequest is something of a codicil, as is appropriate to a man whose life was comprised of a string of apprenticeships and varying occupations but who, to his own surprise, found one day that he had become a "literary person." The strangely independent life of Mark Twain as a cultural icon is nevertheless founded upon his historical profession as an American author. And when one attempts to implicate this same literary person in American literary history, the difficulty is not how to place Mark Twain, but *which* Twain to take up. Twain, as author, personality, and institution, has been divided and subdivided. For all the divisions, however, he mysteriously remains an unfracturable imaginative presence in modern life.

At least since Van Wyck Brooks's *The Ordeal of Mark Twain* it has been fashionable to parcel Twain out, to discover tensions and conflicts in the rich and problematic personality that struck so many contradictory poses: he is a thwarted artist somehow victimized both by his own Western origins and the oppressiveness of Victorian America; he is a man divided against himself, whose dual identity is represented by his given name and his adopted persona; he is both socially constructed and psychically bedeviled. He has been expurgated and emulated, sanitized and bastardized, banned and exalted. And, of course, he has been anthologized. One need only enumerate a few of the titles to indicate how variously available he is to us: *The Family Mark Twain, The Hidden Mark Twain, The Comic Mark Twain Reader, The Birds and Beasts of Mark Twain, Mark Twain: Wit and Wisecracks, A Treasury of Mark Twain, A Pen Warmed Up in Hell.* Doubtless some version of Twain is represented in every American household that keeps books at all. Yet some other portion is likely forbidden entrance.[2]

Scholars and critics have followed him abroad and into his household. They have contemplated his relation to the South, the North, the East, and the West; his relation to his friends and to his relations—to Susy and Orion and Livy and W. D. Howells. They have considered his opinions (and he was a man of inexhaustible opinion) on law, liquor, race, religion, women, history, animals, technology, colonialism, dreams; on the English, the French, the Boers, and the Germans (and, of course, their dreaded language); on Shelley, Scott, Cooper, and Mary Baker Eddy. And they have "placed" him in the literary tradition. Most notably, of course, there is the Mark Twain who serves as the chief exponent of the southwest humor tradition, whose place within and contribution to that same tradition have been exhaustively traced by Walter Blair and others.[3] But there are other Mark Twains: the science fiction writer, the fabulist, the moral philosopher, the dramatist, the satirist, the critic, the lecturer, the prophet and the buffoon, the sage and the literary comedian, the fictionist and the metafictionist.

The literary influence of Twain has developed along manifold lines, prompted varying expressions and forms, and naturally led to different conclusions. One strand of this influence is evident in the straightforward continuation of the adventures of Huck and Tom. Clement Wood's *More Adventures of Huckleberry Finn,* John Seelye's critical and fictional rendering of *The True Adventures of Huckleberry Finn,* Greg Matthews's *The Further Adventures of Huckleberry Finn,* not to mention Twain's own disappointing attempts to extend the exploits of Huck and Tom in *Tom Sawyer, Detective, Tom Sawyer Abroad,* and *Huck Finn*

2. His *1601,* for example, (originally titled *Conversation, as It Was by the Social Fireside, in the Time of the Tudors*) has run through probably one hundred editions, and many of those have been printed by and have changed hands in men's lodges and clubs—as though flatulence in the Queen's Court is really more funny than the blue jay yarn.

3. A succinct but comprehensive view of a feature of the American humor tradition particularly germane to this essay is provided by Blair in "'A Man's Voice, Speaking': A Continuum in American Humor," in *Veins of Humor,* ed. Harry Levin, Harvard English Studies 3 (Cambridge: Harvard University Press, 1972), 185–204.

and Tom Sawyer among the Indians, all these are deliberate sequels and self-conscious extensions of that inheritance.

The technical virtuosity of *Huckleberry Finn* that has become an available resource for other writers marks out another track of Twain's influence. Moreover, the appropriation of Twain's techniques and the detectable thematic similarities between that book and later American writing have in turn become a means to create and understand a portion of American literary history. For such history is made of linkages and affiliations, and in the case of *Huckleberry Finn,* one has a book that other writers have gone to school on; or, as T. S. Eliot put it, Twain discovered in that novel a "new way of writing," valid not only for himself but also for others.[4] The claim may be extravagant. Still, it is difficult to imagine how *To Kill a Mockingbird, Adventures of Augie March, Winesburg, Ohio* or *One Flew Over the Cuckoo's Nest* could have come to be, or at least to have taken quite the same form, had not their creators had the example of *Huckleberry Finn* to draw upon. One may trace a lineage, various as these texts may be, from *Huckleberry Finn* through, say, Sherwood Anderson's "I Want to Know Why" to Faulkner's "The Bear" to Salinger's *Catcher in the Rye* and, finally, to Robert Gover's *The $100 Misunderstanding.* The result is a thematic and stylistic continuity that may or may not pass as a specimen of literary history.

And of course, one may work backward as well. One of the several ironies of the legacy of *Huckleberry Finn* is that a novel which so amusingly calls into question notions of "style" and reverence for received opinion has itself become an aesthetic criterion that may be applied retroactively. Herman Melville's *Redburn,* though it is sometimes forgotten, is narrated by a mere boy, about fifteen years old. As effective as this young narrator's response to a multitude of evils on board the *Highlander* or to the pervasive squalor of Liverpool is, one cannot quite help wondering how Huck might have described them. How wide, one is tempted to ask, might the readership of the *Biglow Papers* be today, had Lowell subtracted from his narrative voices both

---

4. "American Literature and the American Language," *Washington University Studies in Language and Literature* (St. Louis, 1953), 16.

Hosea Biglow and Homer Wilbur and confined himself to the perspective of Birdofredom Sawin? Nor can one help contemplating the very different effects—the pathos, the moral indictment—Rebecca Harding Davis's "Life in the Iron Mills" might have achieved had the Welsh puddler Hugh Wolfe told his own story. Instead, the raw artistic impulse and half-articulate understanding of the world of the ironworker is symbolized in the crude figure in korl rather than embedded and disclosed in the narrative voice itself.

Since the publication of *Huckleberry Finn,* in some fashion, both figurative and real, modern American writers have often enough recognized a kinship between themselves and the boy who modestly sought to tell his own story plainly and directly but who spoke out of a well of ignorance of literary observance and accepted tradition so profound that it amounts to a form of rebellion. And far from suffering from some anxiety of influence, American writers have been rather more anxious than otherwise to claim some portion of the patrimony. For Mark Twain, whatever else he may have offered them, supplied American authors with an image of the author as American.

That image is kaleidoscopically shifty, of course. Even Twain's representation of himself in his *Autobiography* is problematic, and a spate of biographers has attempted to decipher the enigmatic personality with whom we nevertheless confidently claim some acquaintance and intimacy. The several lives of Mark Twain mapped by biographers, fully documented and painstakingly constructed, may seem queer impersonations compared with the Twain that has entered into the public imagination by largely precritical routes. Twain himself, at any rate, banked on the appreciation of what he called his "submerged clientele" and made his direct appeal to the popular mind.

The appearance of familiarity (the seeming democratic availability of the man), combined with fond recollection of the part his imagination of childhood played in many of our own young lives, has helped along the living institution that goes by the same name. However much Samuel Clemens promoted and protected during his lifetime the "Mark Twain" label (itself a registered trademark), after his death the myth has appeared miraculously immune to correction and revision; or rather, the revisions are absorbed into an inviolable and ever larger image that accepts the rebukes and contradictions without pause or diminishment. Mark Twain the institution has acquired increasing momentum in part by the sheer attention it has received and in part by those instruments and individuals that have propelled it forward.

II

One of the most remarkable forums for sustaining and to a degree sanitizing the popular image of Mark Twain that Sam Clemens had invented was the publication of the *Mark Twain Journal* (originally the *Mark Twain Quarterly*). First published in 1936, this journal was to serve as the official publication of the International Mark Twain Society and originated from Webster Groves, Missouri. Though the journal was not exclusively devoted to Mark Twain, its editor, Cyril Clemens, frequently solicited and received endorsements, testimonials, and reminiscences about Mark Twain and his work from every quarter of the globe, from presidents, prime ministers, and potentates, along with appreciative remarks from lesser mortals. The statements were often published in the journal, usually on the front cover. Taken together, whatever their substance, the net effect is of a catalog of what Emmeline Grangerford called "tributes."

The *Mark Twain Journal* did much to consolidate and legitimize the idea that Mark Twain is an indispensable part of American culture, and as if to clinch the point, Cyril Clemens obtained statements from every president from FDR to Richard Nixon, each testifying to an immense admiration of him. For our purposes, however, the most interesting and valuable service Cyril Clemens performed was to extract a multitude of testimonials from important professional writers, several of which were published in his journal. Surely, Mark Twain is the American author most commented upon by other writers. It was in a letter to Cyril Clemens that Willa Cather recalled that she had read *Huckleberry Finn* twenty times; George Bernard Shaw admitted that Mark Twain paved the way for his caustic wit; James Barrie, Edwin Markham, W. B. Yeats, Langston Hughes, and T. S. Eliot confessed to their genuine admiration of him, though for rather different reasons.

In a letter to Clemens, F. Scott Fitzgerald wrote his interesting assessment of *Huckleberry Finn*:

> Huckleberry Finn took the first journey *back*. He was the first to look *back* at the republic from the perspective of the west. His eyes were the first eyes that ever looked at us objectively that were not eyes from overseas. There were mountains at the frontier but he wanted more than mountains to look at with his restless eyes. . . . He wanted to find out about men and how they lived together. And because he turned back we have him forever.[5]

Less familiar is Gertrude Stein's note of appreciation: "Mark Twain, who is as deep and as broad as the Mississippi River and the Mississippi river [sic] is as deep and as broad as a river possibly could be which makes Mark Twain the pleasantest and the most wonderful thing he did and the Mississippi ever might try."[6] Here was a tribute fully in keeping with the populist identity of the journal and worthy of the boast of a Mike Fink—sired by the Missouri hills and dam'd by the Mississippi River, in his turn, Mark Twain created the River itself and made it a common possession.

These and other witnessings for the genius of Twain and, most particularly, for *Adventures of Huckleberry Finn* belong in the company of those testimonials made by American writers but published elsewhere, and, together, they verify a sense of a profound literary inheritance. Yet what, precisely, that inheritance was, and is, remains indefinite. It would have amused Twain himself that he is often

5. The observation was made in a letter in 1935, but it was first published on the cover of the Summer 1965 issue of the *Mark Twain Journal.*

6. The note was given to the Mark Twain Society when Stein was in St. Louis. It was first published on the cover of the Summer 1971 issue of the *Mark Twain Journal.* Alice B. Toklas signed the letter in the margin, apparently as a way of seconding the remarks.

considered a locus and a lens through which we may define literary tradition. For T. S. Eliot the novel was a rarity, and its author ranked with those most un-American writers, Dryden and Swift, as one who had rejuvenated the language, brought it up-to-date and thereby "purified" the dialect of the tribe. For Faulkner and his generation, Anderson and Dreiser were the literary fathers, but Twain was the father of them all, and *Huckleberry Finn* was his best book.[7] As a rule, it seems, American writers were rather anxious to claim a kinship with the orphan boy that the upright citizens from St. Petersburg to Concord had rejected.

Ernest Hemingway's estimate of the novel has become the most memorable and most often cited appraisal, however: "All modern American literature comes from one book by Mark Twain called *Huckleberry Finn.* If you read it you must stop where Nigger Jim is stolen from the boys. That is the real end. The rest is just cheating. But it's the best book we've had. All American writing comes from that. There was nothing before. There has been nothing as good since."[8] Perhaps I am eccentric in detecting something oddly self-serving about the praise. Hemingway's famous remarks are a cluster of unrestrained superlatives—grossly exaggerated, excessive to the point of fawning bad taste, so grandiosely authoritative as to be fatuous. They are a curious, even surreal, blend of the traditionary and the ahistorical: "All American literature comes from one book . . . etc."; it is the "best book we've had . . . etc."; "There was nothing before. There has been nothing as good since."

It is not that Hemingway claims too much, but that he claims more than we can comprehend. *Huckleberry Finn,* he would have us believe, is one bright explosive moment in our literary history— before, was blind groping, the American imagination enslaved to inauthentic, because un-American, custom; after, a falling off and inevitable disappointment and diminishment. He restricts the ines- timable glory of Mark Twain to one novel, and yet, he also advises

7. See respectively Eliot's "American Literature and the American Language," 16– 17, and an interview with William Faulkner by Jean Stein, *Paris Review* (Spring 1956): 46–47.

8. *The Green Hills of Africa* (New York: Charles Scribner's Sons, 1935), 22.

that we do not finish the book, that a full quarter of it is "just cheating."

There is something canny about Hemingway's estimation, however sincere the sentiment. For, in effect, he has taken Twain out of the game altogether. Hawthorne and Melville, Emerson and Thoreau, Dickinson and Whitman (and, after all, it is books, not novels, writing, not fiction, that Hemingway is talking about) become naughts; the Mark Twain of *Huckleberry Finn* becomes an infinite. What remains, is . . . well, Hemingway perhaps. Still, there is something profoundly accurate about the remark as well. *Adventures of Huckleberry Finn* is not merely the object of scrutiny and interpretation; it has become the means by which we measure and come to understand much of American writing. Hemingway's appropriation and refinement of the example of that novel is well known, yet it may be that the example he himself supplies blinds us to other features of Twain's legacy.

Such at least was the opinion of Ralph Ellison who, in "Twentieth-Century Fiction and the Black Mask of Humanity," observed that Huck's decision to help Jim to freedom (a decision that marks him as wicked and condemned to hell) represents Twain's full acceptance of his own responsibility in the existing social order and condition. This, says Ellison, is the "tragic face" behind the comic mask of Huckleberry Finn. This is also what, in his estimation, has largely disappeared in the work of modern American writers. In the case of Hemingway, the writer appropriated Twain's technical innovations but missed or declined the moral vision the technique was meant to dramatize.[9] The consequences, not just for Hemingway but for American literature, are significant: "Thus what for Twain was a means to a moral end became for Hemingway an end in itself. And just as the trend toward technique for the sake of technique and production for the sake of the market lead to the neglect of the human need out of which they spring, so do they lead in literature to

9. In *Mark Twain: An American Prophet* (Boston: Houghton Mifflin Co., 1970) Maxwell Geismar makes the same point as Ellison, less charitably perhaps, but far more succinctly: "It is curious incidentally that Hemingway, who derived so much from Mark Twain's prose, learned so little from his spirit" (372–73).

a marvelous technical virtuosity won at the expense of a gross insensitivity to fraternal values."[10]

Clearly, the acceptance of this responsibility in the case of a man like Twain, who tended to suffer from guilty feelings over events he could not possibly control and whose imagination often exceeded his deliberate purpose, is a complicated one. Nevertheless, Ellison's insight into the social responsibility of the novelist has its inexact parallels in Twain's inner life, and it points to a significant feature of his imaginative presence in our own time. To appropriate the narrative device of telling a story from the point of view of someone who does not fully comprehend the humor of his expression or the gravity of his experience, but who is nonetheless able to suggest some indefinite *dis*-ease about that world, opens up innumerable possibilities for the novelist. But, finally, the force of those narratives depends less upon technique than upon the capacity to fully imagine the life and inherent dignity of another. This is but another way of saying what James M. Cox has already said: "If the 'incorrect' vernacular of *Huckleberry Finn* is to be more than décor, it must enact an equally 'incorrect' vision. Otherwise, the style becomes merely a way of saying rather than a way of being."[11]

Fully half the achievement of *Huckleberry Finn* lies, I believe, in Twain's remarkable and quite momentary ability to so completely identify himself with Huck's interior life that he was able to give that figure voice, often at the expense of his own conscious literary intentions. What is submerged beneath the vernacular observations of this outcast boy is not solely an adult satire or the private complaints and disenchantments of the author. Nor is the novel merely imaginative indulgence in the freedoms and freshness of childhood. In addi-

10. "Twentieth-Century Fiction and the Black Mask of Humanity," in *Shadow and Act* (New York: New American Library, 1966), 52. When Ellison's essay was first published in *Confluence* (December 1953), he asked that an editorial note be included that indicated that it was written just after the war and reflected the "bias and shortsightedness" he felt at the time. Such bias is certainly understandable when an African-American observes, as so many had after that and other wars, that the patriotism of minorities, upon which the republic depended during a national emergency, was a negligible consideration when white America went back to business as usual.

11. *Mark Twain: The Fate of Humor* (Princeton: Princeton University Press, 1966), 176.

tion, there is the fully felt complicity in the social and emotional condition of his created characters.

In modern fiction, often the same narrative technique masks the author's felt presence and achieves what we have come to admire as aesthetic detachment. By contrast, what is remarkable about *Huckleberry Finn* is that Twain so committed himself to the lifeworld of his young outcast and, later, his black companion. It is true that Twain's disguised grievances and yearnings are imbedded in the narrative as well. What is also masked, however, is a sense of his own implication and guilt in the prevailing hurt and tyranny that is the social world of the novel. Twain's creative impulses no doubt began in the simple desire to escape the cares of the adult world, but life along the Mississippi became a recalcitrant world of its own that was not to be displaced by the figures of the imagination or sheer technical skill. Perhaps the severest test of the realist writer lies not so much in looking on life directly but in taking the risk that life as it is imaginatively depicted may return the gaze and make it known that it has formed its own independent measurements and judgments of the author. Eventually, when Twain's creation stood as accusation and plea to the creator, he did not retreat from the responsibility.

My point here is that there is some evidence to suggest not only that Ellison is perhaps right about the course of American fiction and the too easy forfeiture of an acute moral vision, but also that Twain reveals poignantly and by snatches the subconscious costs such responsibility may exact and the pain and courage it may require to disclose, even covertly, a personal stake in the prevailing social ethos of the country.[12] There is a further point implicit in Ellison's observa-

---

12. Needless to say, Twain is not exempt from the charge of retreat from contaminations of the political and social fabric of the republic. In letters, he sometimes insisted that the first responsibility of citizenship was to keep "clean"; in *A Connecticut Yankee* he averred that the primary obligation of the individual was to preserve some "atom" of self and let the rest land in "Sheol"; in my essay "Life Imitating Art," reprinted above, I have argued that in "The Private History of a Campaign That Failed" Twain sought to justify his own "desertion" not only from the Confederate Army but also from an active involvement in the fate of the nation. In *Huckleberry Finn,* however, and mostly through an exploration of the character of Jim and Huck's complex relation to him, Twain divested himself of the role of comic satirist safely

tions and one, perhaps, worth developing. It is unimaginable, not to say intolerable, to divorce the literary *manner* of, say, Dr. Johnson, or Voltaire, from his literary *matter.* Their style and moral vision are inseparably fused. Not so, it seems, with Mark Twain.

III

Quite apart from the liability that the reader may dismiss the serious intent of comedy, a risk that any humorist runs, Twain's technical achievements and improvisations in *Huckleberry Finn* are also and all too easily detachable from what Howells described as the strong tide of moral earnestness in the man, and from the creative energy that gave birth to this new way of writing. By way of illustration, we might linger over the example of Ring Lardner; for in him we have a figure whose talents invited comparisons with Twain, but whose achievements, though considerable, failed (as Ellison says Hemingway failed) to take full advantage of a rich double legacy.

Ernest Hemingway no doubt detected in Huck's account of his experiences the submerged hurt and confusion of a boy who had witnessed far more than he could articulate or even cared to remember, but who naively disclosed a portion of a sensibility from which the rest could clearly be inferred and felt. It remained for Hemingway in his own work to convey, often brilliantly, a precarious sense of woundedness and conflict that owes something to Twain's example. In Sherwood Anderson, too, one can sense an allegiance to a path marked out by *Huckleberry Finn,* his favorite book by his favorite author. Often Anderson's masterly evocations are of events witnessed or overheard precisely at a time when the narrating mind vaguely realized that they were important, but whose subsequent telling is nagged into existence by the very perplexity they have since engendered. These storyteller's stories are powerful because

---

above the objects of his contempt and began to develop themes that were bound to recoil upon him, not only as an individual but also as a citizen.

they render the effort to comprehend something the reader understands all the more forcefully by the pained artlessness of the narration. However, his narrators' recollections often soften into mere regret (as in "The Triumph of the Egg") or lament (as in "I'm a Fool"). Sometimes they reveal a dark and half-mystical naturalism (as in "A Death in the Woods"). Anderson's absurdities frequently serve not so much as comic correctives as they diagnose pathologies or picture for the reader the disturbingly blighted lives of what Anderson called "grotesques."

Hemingway and Anderson freely acknowledged their debts to Twain, but in the early years of the century it was Ring Lardner who was, in many minds, the heir apparent to the author of *Huckleberry Finn*. In 1924, Edmund Wilson asked, "Will Ring Lardner, then, go on to his *Huckleberry Finn* or has he already told all he knows?" One never knows, he concedes, but Lardner benefits from Twain's same freedom of view and approaches his fictions with a "perceptive interest in human beings instead of with a naturalist's formula." For Sherwood Anderson, in 1919, Lardner was a "word fellow, one who cares about the words of our American speech and who is perhaps doing more than any other American to give new force to the words of our everyday life." But his artistic devotion might also conceal some secret hurt that he carried within him, some "shy hungry child" that did not risk exposure. This covering up is forgivable if "he is really using his talent for sympathetic understanding of life, if in secret he is being another Mark Twain and working in secret on his own *Huckleberry Finn*." At any rate, for Anderson, not even Twain had a "more sensitive understanding of the fellow in the street, in the hooch joint, the ball-park, and the city suburb." And in 1924, H. L. Mencken also invited comparison with Twain, but he worried that Lardner would be lost to contemporary neglect, that his special vernacular talents would sink beneath the weight of their own particularity of reference. In other words, Mencken feared that Lardner's greatest ally, American speech itself, would move on its own devious course and leave Lardner's vernacular trapped in a linguistic past beyond retrieval by later generations.[13]

13. See respectively, Wilson, "Mr. Lardner's American Characters," *Dial* (July

In the 1920s the comparisons to Twain were probably justified, but Lardner had already refused them. "I wouldn't consider Mark Twain our greatest humorist," he told an interviewer in 1917. "I guess George Ade is. Certainly he appeals to us more than Mark Twain does because he belongs to our own time." Lardner, as a man of his own time, confessed that he knew of the life and characters Twain described only by "hearsay." He admires Twain's fiction, but he prefers Tarkington's Penrod stories. "I've known Booth Tarkington's boys and I've not known those of Mark Twain. Mark Twain's boys are tough and poverty stricken and they belong to a period very different from that of our own boys. But we all know Penrod and his boys."[14] It is common to turn Lardner's words against him, to argue that his privileged upbringing in Niles, Michigan, deprived him of the larger democratic sympathies that animated Twain's creations. There is something to this, of course, but the relative social distance between Lardner and his created characters (his nurses, boxers, barbers, and baseball players) is no greater than the distance between Twain and Pap Finn, Aunt Rachel, or the king and the duke.

Nor can it be convincingly maintained that Lardner did not enjoy the same literary opportunities provided by his own historical mo-

1924): 69–72; Anderson, "Four American Impressions: Gertrude Stein, Paul Rosenfeld, Ring Lardner, Sinclair Lewis," in *The Portable Sherwood Anderson,* ed. Horace Gregory, revised edition (New York: Viking Penguin, 1972), 430–31; and Mencken, "Lardner," in *Prejudices: A Selection,* ed. James T. Farrell (New York: Vintage Books, 1958), 197–201. Mencken's fears point to another aspect of Twain's legacy. Despite his own appreciative remarks about Lardner in *The American Language,* it is quite true that much of Lardner is lost to the contemporary reader. Mencken worried that the shifting historical course of the American language might trap Lardner in his own time and later generations would serve him up, if at all, "as a sandwich between introduction and notes." This last remark is insightful, but not so much because Mencken's disdain of the "perfesser" is warranted. Instead, the American speech that Twain transcribed was also broadcast throughout the world from the lecture platform, and a host of Twain imitators have since sustained our familiarity with a language that has long since passed from the scene. In addition, Lardner has not enjoyed the special labors of scholars (particularly Robert Ramsay and Frances Emerson) to preserve that speech. In a word, there is no *Ring Lardner Lexicon* as there is a *Mark Twain Lexicon.*

14. "Three Stories a Year Are Enough for a Writer," *New York Times Magazine,* March 25, 1917, 44.

ment. His literary career as journalist, fiction writer, and dramatist spanned an era as rich in material ripe for exploitation and satire as the 1880s and 1890s. The Progressive era and the aftermath of the Great War manifested their enthusiasms, disappointments, and sentimental excesses in different ways, but Lardner was alert to the thickening complications and intricacies that were so rapidly changing the direction of American life—the abandonment of rural and pastoral prerogatives in favor of urban excitements; the nervous entrance into the community of nations on equal terms; and the rhetoric of confidence and opportunity uttered in the face of debilitating poverty and prejudice, irresistible social stratification, and the incomprehensible reticulations of social existence.

There was a richness of literary possibility available to such an intelligence as his—outrageous ironies and absurdities, American originals in the speakeasy and the dugout, and a multitude of American languages and dialects that he might faithfully transcribe. Lardner's Alibi Ike, for example, in his own way, belongs in the company of Scotty Briggs and Jim Blaine as someone comically unaware of his hilarious effects upon both his companions and his readers. The difference is that Twain catches his figures at a precise moment (Scotty in the unaccustomed presence of the parson and Jim Blaine in a state of perfect and "symmetrical" drunkenness); one can imagine them functioning profitably and comfortably on other occasions. However, Alibi Ike's proliferating and inexhaustible fund of excuses marks him as someone whose own considerable gifts and modest affections not only will always be cause for begrudging amusement, but also will likewise keep him outside the community whose admiration and acceptance he so urgently desires.

In his most famous story, "Haircut," Lardner reveals, through the barber narrator's recitation and headshaking and amused assent to the cruel adventures of Jim Kendall, a survival of the Bricksville crew in modern American life. The violence, laziness, coarseness, and vast indifference of the community are confided to the patron by a vernacular narrator who discloses more about himself and his town than he knows. Kendall gets his comeuppance at last—a literal-minded, half-wit boy, Paul Dickson, shoots and kills him. However it is idiocy, not innocence, that corrects the mischief and rights the moral imbalance, and one can hardly find consoling affirmations in this fact.

The life of Midge Kelly in "Champion" is a very unfunny restatement of Twain's "Story of the Bad Little Boy." Like Twain's bad boy, Midge abuses his mother, strikes his siblings, cheats his friends, and yet prospers—he becomes a champion prizefighter. Kelly's self-absorbed callousness and cruelty are more active and pernicious and therefore more sinister, however. The reason lies, I think, not in the character's violent profession but in the author's tone and narrative detachment, in the easy acceptance of the Midge Kellys of the world as brutal and incontestable facts of social existence.

At the other end of the scale are Lardner's nonsense plays, hilariously unactable and unproducible absurdist dramas. (One of his stage directions reads: *The curtain is lowered for seven days to denote the lapse of a week.*") At times, as in "Gaspiri (The Upholsterers)," they are reminiscent of Twain's "Encounter with an Interviewer":

> *First Stranger* Where was you born?
> *Second Stranger* Out of wedlock.
> *First Stranger* That's a mighty pretty country around there.
> *Second Stranger* Are you married?
> *First Stranger* I don't know. There's a woman living with me, but I can't place her.[15]

In Lardner, too, there is an originality of experimentation and imaginative conception that rivals Twain's. His humor owed more to "literary humorists" such as Artemus Ward and Petroleum Nasby, however, than it did to the coarser and more ribald tradition of Thorpe's Jim Doggett or Hooper's Simon Suggs. Nevertheless, like Twain, he extended the range of the vernacular comedy when he applied it to the epistolary form inherited from Richardson instead of to the picaresque tradition that Twain had adopted in *Huck Finn*.

15. *The Ring Lardner Reader,* ed. Maxwell Geismar (New York: Charles Scribner's Sons, 1963), 602.

This occurred in 1916 when he collected his Jack Keefe stories and published the first of his Busher novels, *You Know Me, Al.*

Bold as the experiment was, however, it shifted the vernacular away from the sources of oral tradition in a way that committed the author to a different kind of humor, one that might enlist our pity but was not likely to enlarge our sympathies. For, as James Cox has so elegantly shown, Jack's ungrammaticality reveals in the narrative consciousness an "unassimilated correctness" and an "abortive formality";[16] Jack strains for acceptability, but we his readers are first aware of his awkwardness and self-consciousness at the level of language. The predictable result of this shift is a certain enforced condescension established in the reader. Huck is fleeing social usage; thus, the apt lack of restraint in his language. Huck's readers, because we like his company, follow him in wish and imagination. Jack Keefe, by contrast, so desires admittance into a social order and community (whose terms are implicitly defined by the linguistic correctness he continually violates) that his constantly renewed efforts only further defeat his purposes. More to the point, because Lardner's comedy cannot function in the absence of an unstated but thoroughly understood social and linguistic propriety, to laugh at all means that we must laugh at the narrator, not through him.

What in Huck Finn is innocence becomes in Jack Keefe debilitating ignorance. Huck's self-deprecation is transformed in Jack to exasperating self-deception. Interestingly, because Huck is a child who has never had a childhood, we have access to a laughable and contemptible world in which his youthful point of view supplies a perspective that is more mature than the adult world Huck cannot fully understand. Jack Keefe, by contrast, is a man-child who does not know how to grow up. His fears are translated into "manly" boasts and threats followed hard and fast by accommodation, chop logic, and extenuation, comic gestures of self-protection and self-exposure. Keefe's misspellings and malapropisms are the verbal equivalent to his social maladjustments, and far from supplying his narra-

16. See "Toward Vernacular Humor," *Virginia Quarterly Review* 46 (Spring 1970), especially 321–25.

tive with vernacular lyricism they mark him as a yokel and easy amusement to all around him.

At times, one almost feels that if Jack could correct his grammar, he could correct his life. But Jack Keefe is immersed in and controlled by a world of contracts, wavers, and lawsuits (for "none support"), a world of language so far beyond him that his own vernacular projections of self only announce his failure and acquiescence. His letters home to Bedford, to the Al who knows him so well, are letters of confused desperation. They come from Chicago and Philadelphia and New York, cities that are eating him alive, but it is clear he will never get to that little yellow house back in Bedford. He wants, by way of compensation for his real losses, to contrive imaginary gains, to be the hero of his own life, if only for his pal back home. What prevents even so momentary a satisfaction, one senses, is his inability to displace the real world with a vividly imagined one. His powers of self-absorption and self-deception are great, but there is no commensurate imaginative faculty or confident verbal facility that might displace the real world that presses in on him. Like Tom Sawyer, Jack has romantic illusions, but, unlike him, he has no joyful sense of playing a part. Like Huck, Jack has a vernacular perspective on events, but, unlike him, his language limits his world and insures his victimage. Even in his preconcerted boasts, his words recoil upon him: "Some man stopped me and asked me did I want to go to a show. He said he had a ticket. I asked him what show and he said the Follies. I never heard of it but I told him I would go if he had a ticket to spare. He says I will spare you this one for three dollars. I says You must take me for some boob. He says No I wouldn't insult no boob. So I walks on but if he had of insulted me I would of busted him."[17] His sentiments and attempts to cope are annihilated by the same language that serves to communicate his hurt and pride:

> It is all off between Violet and I. She wasn't the sort of girl I suspected. She is just like them all Al. No heart. I wrote her a letter from Chicago telling her I was sold to San Francisco and she wrote back a postcard saying something about not haveing no time to

17. *You Know Me, Al: A Busher's Letters* (1916) (New York: Vintage Books, 1984), 66.

waste on bushers. What do you know about that Al? Calling me a busher. I will show them. She wasn't no good Al and I figure I am well rid of her. Good riddance is rubbish as they say.[18]

These comic deflations and distortions amuse but they don't provoke. Lardner's vernacular is not mere ornament; it is integral to the fabric of his fiction and his artistic purpose. What is disturbing, however, is that there is a bite and sting without apparent aim or direction, an unmistakable satirical impulse without a comprehensible satirical object. In the absence of a clearly inferable moral norm, the comedy recurs to the purely arbitrary norm of social usage, including the standard English usage Keefe so comically manhandles and mangles. Unlike the typical reaction to Huck, our comic understanding of the Busher does not serve as a link between our sympathies and a larger awareness of the human spectacle. Quite the contrary, our pity and amusement are additional insults to his confused condition.

Simply put, psychologically, morally, and emotionally, Ring Lardner's Jack Keefe is not the descendant of Huckleberry Finn but the country cousin of J. Alfred Prufrock. The Busher is in fact Prufrock in a jersey and cleats. What separates Huck and Jack in the imagination is not so much attributable to differences in artistic perception, genre, or craft as it is the inevitable result of enlisting the vernacular to perform the detached analysis of the interior life instead of to examine the fate of the republic and the moral constitution of its citizens. If the writer is to adopt a vernacular narrator the reader is to take seriously, then sooner or later he or she must also adopt certain democratic sympathies and endorse certain fraternal values implicit in the register of the narrative voice itself.

The same artistic detachment that is likely to be praised in one quarter (in Eliot or Hemingway or Joyce) is cause, in another, for complaint. Clifton Fadiman, for instance, has insisted that Lardner's fiction is motivated by a "triangle of hate," and that the resulting product is a cold-blooded misanthropy. The judgment is no doubt too severe. Ring Lardner was an exquisite craftsman and a great

18. Ibid., 53.

humorist, but the resources of Twain's technique, isolated from a concern with a larger social vision come soon enough to appear as mere cagey evasions or, worse, a string of one-liners. When the writer possesses a vernacular vision but no special gifts for dialect, however, an indebtedness to Twain's example will likely go unnoticed. This is the case with Willa Cather.

IV

At first glance, any comparison of Willa Cather to Mark Twain must seemed strained, perhaps farfetched. One of the few people ever to propose a fundamental connection between these two is Eudora Welty. Cather and the Twain of *Huckleberry Finn,* she observed, "stand together in *bigness.*" In their "sense of it, their authority over it" they share only this similarity: "they are totally unlike except in their greatest respects, except in being about something big."[19] Surely it is not vastness of scene or profound purpose Welty detected in them, but some sure artistic commitment to a palpable yet transcendentally authorizing ideal that dignifies their respective heroes. Huckleberry Finn and Ántonia Shimerda or Alexandra Bergson are small people, really, smaller still measured against the extent of the Mississippi River or the breadth of the Nebraska sky. But there is a homey grandeur to them as well, as if the river and the sky deferred to their presence or tended to their needs. In this "greatest respect" Twain and Cather belong together. But there are more tangible links as well.

Cather's admiration of Twain is familiar. For her, there were only three American novels that had the possibility of a long, long life: *The Scarlet Letter, Adventures of Huckleberry Finn,* and *The Country of the Pointed Firs.* "I can think of no others that confront time and change so serenely," she wrote. Later generations, she predicted, will come upon these works and exclaim, a "masterpiece." The thrill of sudden

19. "The House of Willa Cather," reprinted in *Critical Essays on Willa Cather,* ed. John J. Murphy (Boston: G. K. Hall and Co., 1984), 73.

discovery will be as Frost's mower who discovers in the afternoon a tuft of meadow flowers the mower in the morning had spared and will gaze upon it and wonder. The poise and serenity she discerned in these three novels will speak to the future and supply "the one message that even the scythe of Time spares."[20]

In a letter to Cyril Clemens, Cather recalled an encounter with a Russian violinist in Paris. He had grown up along a river too, and he told her that ever since he had read a Russian translation of *Huckleberry Finn* he had wanted to see the Mississippi, a river that must be even more wonderful and romantic than the Volga. Cather questioned the man about the novel, a bit skeptical that it could have had such an effect on him. He remembered it perfectly. "But how in the world could the talk of Nigger Jim be translated into Russian?" she wondered.

> And what would become of the seven shadings of Southern dialect which the author in his preface tells the reader must not be confounded one with the other? It seemed to me that the most delightful things in "Huckleberry Finn" must disappear in a translation. One could easily translate Parkman or Emerson, certainly: but how translate Mark Twain? The only answer seems to be that if a book has vitality enough, it can live through even the brutalities of translators.[21]

Cather's recorded reactions to *Huckleberry Finn* are interesting because they identify and value features of the novel that are sometimes missed. First, in her estimation, the best work of Hawthorne, Jewett, and Twain escape the contingencies of time and the modifications of taste. The remark is all the more interesting since *The Scarlet Letter, Adventures of Huckleberry Finn* and, in its own special way, *The Country of the Pointed Firs* are all historical novels, but historical novels with a difference. Cather made the distinction between

20. See *Willa Cather on Writing: Critical Studies on Writing as an Art* (New York: Alfred A. Knopf, 1949), 58.

21. A facsimile of the undated letter with the author's corrections and deletions (which are not reproduced in the above quotation) is printed on the back cover of the *Mark Twain Journal* 15 (Winter 1973–1974).

historical novels (such as Flaubert's *Salammbô*) that regard the past from the privileged vantage point of the present and thereby acquire a certain condescension toward their subjects, and those (such as Thomas Mann's Joseph novels) that explore the material from behind, as it were, as though the characters were not foregone conclusions, whose lives instead were made of choices and whose motives were projections into a future of hope and possibility. Surely, that is a quality that characterizes *Huckleberry Finn* and, perhaps, that is also what Roy Harvey Pearce is getting at when he points out that Huck is trapped in his book, that he forever exists as a possibility, not an actuality.[22] It also happens to be the quality that Cather sought to achieve in her own historical novels, particularly in the best of them, *Death Comes for the Archbishop*.

The second observation, derived from her conversation with the Russian violinist, implies that *Huckleberry Finn* thrives on a quality and vitality of feeling that is not only apart from the density of its dialect but stronger even than the inevitable butcheries of translation. This second point is a correlative of the first. If works of the imagination are to escape history, they must also escape the bondage of language. In her most familiar essay, "The Novel Démeublé," she speaks elegantly on this point: "Whatever is felt upon the page without being specifically named there—that, one might say, is created. It is the inexplicable presence of the thing not named, of the overtone divined by the ear but not heard by it, the verbal mood, the emotional aura of the fact or the thing or the deed, that gives high quality to the novel or the drama as well as to poetry itself."[23]

Huckleberry Finn is dense with what Henry James called "the solidity of specification," and especially dense in its attachment to the

22. See "Yours Truly, Huck Finn," in *One Hundred Years of "Huckleberry Finn": The Boy, His Book, and American Culture; Centennial Essays*, ed. Robert Sattelmeyer and J. Donald Crowley (Columbia: University of Missouri Press, 1985), 313–24. Pearce's essay, along with Cather's observations about the historical novel and her own example of the genre, might prove instructive to New Historicists who typically regard texts as socially and linguistically constructed artifacts. Some texts, and *Huckleberry Finn* is one, drive beyond historical contingency precisely because their impulsions and art drive beyond the condition of language itself.

23. *Willa Cather on Writing,* 41.

precise rendering of American speech, but its dialect only solidifies the verbal mood established in the reader. Pap Finn is a living character, not because he speaks a historically conditioned language, but because his bigotry and ranting speech is still poisonous to the ear. Like a figure from Bunyan's *Pilgrim's Progress,* Pap is a deputy for baseness itself; his truest idiom is brute and degrading ignorance. We hear his words, but we divine his presence.

Cather, however, did not possess Twain's gift for dialect, and she seems to have known it. Nevertheless, in 1913, when she accepted her native Nebraska material in her novel *O Pioneers!,* she "hit the home pasture" and discovered, as Twain had discovered in the return to the experience of his youth along the Mississippi, a sudden liberation of the imagination. And, like her narrator Jim Burden in *My Ántonia,* she came to believe that it would be a fine thing to be the first to bring the muse into one's own country. Sooner or later, she remarked, the writer rediscovers the material of one's birth and circumstance, material that, because it is typically taken for granted, produces no special excitement or interest. But when the "inner feeling" of the familiar mysteriously shapes itself on the page and supplants the purely writerly desire to build "external stories," then the writer will have resumed "his one really precious possession."[24]

Cather often observed that a writer's authentic experience, and thus her most valuable literary material, is acquired before the age of fifteen, and she was fond of quoting the advice Sarah Orne Jewett once offered to her: "Of course, one day you will write about your own country. In the meantime, get all you can. One must know the world *so well* before one can know the parish."[25] It was Jewett who provided the example of the writer who wrote about her own country unashamedly and with what Cather once called the "gift of sympathy," but Twain's example must have served her as well. Certainly the dignity and respect with which Twain treats Huck and Jim were qualities she might admire and emulate. At any rate, Cather

24. See the "Preface" to *Alexander's Bridge,* new edition, (Boston: Houghton Mifflin, 1922), v–ix.
25. Ibid., vii.

was especially proud that, in *O Pioneers!,* she had created for the first time in American fiction Swedish characters who were not portrayed as lumpish buffoons.

Cather's admiration of *Huckleberry Finn* is there plainly enough, but the impress of his influence or the mark of his peculiar gifts is difficult to locate in her own work. Her fiction by no means participates in the traditions of American humor. In fact, unless one has inspected her letters (in which she reveals a comic wit and vivacity and, at times, wholesome self-parody), one is apt to conclude that she is much like the undertaker at the Wilks funeral, with no more smile to her than a ham. And unless one is familiar with her early criticism, there is little ground to suspect a barbed, even malicious, satiric wit. Particularly in her early fiction (as in "The Willing Muse" or "The Garden Lodge"), one finds the comedy of situation but no particular inclination to exploit the latent humor of it. In sum, in Willa Cather one has a writer who has a vernacular vision but no extraordinary vernacular capabilities.

Her kinship with Twain is detectable almost entirely in her eventual discovery that the land and people of her youth were worthy of literary treatment. Ántonia Shimerda, Nancy Till, Spanish Johnny, Aunt Tillie, Alexandra Bergson, old Rosicky, and so many others are vernacular characters, but Cather had to find extravernacular means to convey a richness and interest of personality and purpose that might so easily degenerate into mere comedy of language. Her Czechs, Poles, Germans, and Swedes are typically immigrants or first-generation Americans. They, like their spoken English, are rendered awkward by the process of assimilation and accommodation to a new country and a new language. Unlike Twain's characters, however, Cather's immigrants are trying to speak alike and not succeeding. Beneath the hard consonants and hesitant cadences, however, is fierce pride and fluent intelligence. But how to convey these qualities she so much admired in the Nebraska neighbors of her youth? Her usual solution to this problem is brilliantly simple—she avoids the difficulty altogether.

It is true that her characters sometimes speak their own language, but they are seldom if ever capable of speaking their own world.

Consider, for example, Frank Shabata, in *O Pioneers!:* "I never mean to do not'ing to dat boy. I ain't had not'ing ag'in dat boy. I always like dat boy fine." Cather's vernacular speech is perfectly adequate, but it is unequal to the quality of feeling the author has for the characters themselves. However, she found other means to convey human personality without sacrificing the felt quality of speech. For example, after Frank's protestation in the passage above, he says, "I forget English. We not talk here [prison], except swear."[26] More often, as in the speech of Spanish Johnny or Wünsch in *The Song of the Lark,* she inserts into their otherwise standard English dialogue Spanish or German phrases (often song lyrics or proverbs) in order to suggest linguistic as well as rich historical and cultural difference.

Cather is ever alert to the social force of language throughout her fiction. In *The Song of the Lark,* we are told that Mrs. Kronborg spoke Swedish to her sisters and colloquial English to her neighbors. Her daughter Thea, "who had a rather sensitive ear, until she went to school never spoke at all except in monosyllables."[27] More often still, the narrator serves as translator in the manner that Hemingway adopted some time later in *For Whom the Bell Tolls.* In *O Pioneers!* the narrator notes that Ivar, whom the neighbors consider queer, even crazy, "never learned to speak English and his Norwegian was quaint and grave, like the speech of the more old-fashioned people." Following this explanation, Ivar speaks: "Mistress, . . . the folk have been looking coldly at me of late. You know there has been talk."[28] His helpless dignity is registered at the level of cadence and syntax instead of at the level of diction.

Only twice does Cather use a first-person narrator whose youth and limited comprehension bear the marks of Huck Finn, and in both instances it is sensibility, not dialect, that invites the comparison. In *My Mortal Enemy,* she has a young woman named Nellie Birdseye tell the story of the sophisticated and beautiful Myra Henshawe. When they first meet, the young Nellie receives instruction on dress and

26. *O Pioneers!* (Boston: Houghton Mifflin Co., 1913), 293–94.
27. *The Song of the Lark,* revised edition (Boston: Houghton Mifflin Co., 1932), 20.
28. *O Pioneers!,* 90–91.

manner at a time when her interest in the allurements that will make her a woman are paramount. But as the years go by, it becomes apparent that Myra Henshawe's life is utter repudiation of those same things that made her so interesting to the young woman. Myra's husband, Oswald, somehow preserves the original love and vitality of feeling he first felt for his wife throughout the subtractions of age and impoverishment. The distressing result is that Oswald becomes his wife's "mortal enemy," a reminder of her lost youth and beauty and station, and in the end she turns from him to tend her rosary and die by the sea. The novel is a devastating study of marriage as an institution and love as a force that ends in contempt. The narrator understands but little of this, however, and her limitations only make the tale more disturbingly poignant.

Less bitter, if no less effective, is "Two Friends." It begins: "Even in early youth, when the mind is so eager for the new and untried, while it is still a stranger to faltering and fear, we yet like to think that there are certain unalterable realities, somewhere at the bottom of things. These anchors may be ideas; but more often they are merely pictures, vivid memories, which in some unaccountable and very personal way give us courage." For the unnamed narrator, that anchor is the friendship she observes in Mr. Dillon and Mr. Trueman. These men have little in common. The first is an Irish Catholic, a Democrat, and a banker; the second a Protestant, a Republican, and a rancher. But for the thirteen-year-old child who plays jacks on the boardwalk along the brick wall where the two meet to chat every evening, there is something precious and valuable in their casual conversation. It is talk she no longer recalls and at the time did not understand except for the quality of voice that engaged in it. Of Dillon, she remembers, "Every sentence he uttered was alive, never languid, perfunctory, slovenly, unaccented. When he made a remark, it not only meant something, but sounded like something,—sounded like the thing he meant."[29]

She listens to these two men who reveal to her quite accidentally, and more in the quality of the voice than in anything else, "the

29. In *Obscure Destinies* (1932) (New York: Vintage Books, 1974), 193, 206.

strong bracing reality of successful, large-minded men who had made their way in the world when business was still a personal adventure."[30] But when Dillon travels to Chicago and becomes enthusiastic by the bloated rhetoric of Bryant's "Cross of Gold" speech, he returns to her small town a changed man. His voice becomes shrill, convinced of its mission. It becomes unnatural. The end of the friendship is at hand: it dissolves in a "quarrel of principle." No degree of self-interest could have damaged this friendship, the narrator believes. Political ideology and rhetoric despise affection and destroy its attachments.

For the child the loss is a permanent regret. Much older, the scar of that ruptured friendship is still tender to the narrator who as a child admired it as a truth in the world. And when at odd moments it is touched by accidental circumstance, "it rouses the old uneasiness; the feeling of something broken that could so easily have been mended; of something delightful that was senselessly wasted, of a truth that was accidentally distorted—one of the truths we want to keep."[31]

"Two Friends" was written in 1931, and perhaps Cather was responding to a multitude of fallen friendships occasioned by the Depression and "quarrels of principle" over the several political strategies advanced to repair the economy. At any rate, by most any reckoning, Willa Cather's own political conservatism must seem quaint, amusing, even touching. She opposed FDR's New Deal, but she sent money and packages back to folks in Webster County, Nebraska, who were having a rough go of it. During World War II, she was more encouraged by the fact that they were still giving concerts in bomb-torn London than by Patton's military triumphs. But her own social vision was grounded in bigness—in the old truths of friendship, desire, and courage, enabling attachments which are prior to political commitment. In that greatest respect, Cather also resembles Mark Twain.

In one of his boldest imaginative experiments, Twain pits the comprehensive and repressive political structures of the Church and

---

30. In ibid., 218.
31. In ibid., 230.

a feudal economy against Hank Morgan's technological innovation and progressive social engineering. The result is comic disaster, culminating in the Battle of the Sand Belt. But the novel ends with a delirious Hank reaching out across the centuries for his wife, Sandy, and his daughter, Hello Central. And in *Huckleberry Finn,* it is the sound heart in an ignorant boy that, however briefly, defeats the powerful claims of civilized society. Cather's *Death Comes for the Archbishop* ends with Archbishop Latour facing death with equanimity and poise, but his thoughts are not on eternity but the beginnings of lifelong association and friendship with Joseph Vaillant. Alexandra Bergson's story ends with the prediction of her death: "Fortunate country, that is one day to receive hearts like Alexandra's into its bosom, to give them out again in the yellow wheat, in the rustling corn, in the shining eyes of youth!"[32] For Jim Burden, Ántonia's face and gestures "somehow reveal the meaning in common things"; she lent herself "to immemorial human attitudes which we recognize by instinct as universal and true."[33]

Eudora Welty once observed that there is no "middle distance" in Cather's best work. Instead of the dense complexities of social life and political compromise, there is the broad sweep of time and space and a handful of human figures whose lives are dignified in common things. This is the portion of Huck's legacy Cather claimed for her characters. For Langston Hughes's Jesse B. Semple, such a life is unavailable, the middle distance of the color line crowds in upon him. Simple confronts it not with serenity and poise but with comic wit and intelligent complaint, and the result is a latter day vernacular hero.

V

While it is true that Langston Hughes read and admired *Huckleberry Finn,*[34] the question of a literary inheritance derived from a

---

32. *O Pioneers!,* 309.
33. *My Ántonia* (1918) (Boston: Houghton Mifflin Co., 1954), 353.
34. According to Arnold Rampersad, in *The Life of Langston Hughes,* vol. 1, *1902–*

white writer (whose own racial attitudes are more than a little problematic) is particularly complicated.[35] Still, Hughes was gratified by the critic Ben Lehman's observation that Hughes's Jesse Semple (more familiarly known as "Simple") was a worthy successor to the comic creations of Mark Twain: "I'd not thought of it before myself," Hughes responded. "But [I] am glad if there's something of the same quality there, naturally."[36] The remark is aptly phrased, for Hughes neither denies nor affirms a correspondence between his created character and his humor and those of Mark Twain; if there is the happy accident of broad appeal and analogous humorous effects, so much the better. Though he became a Knight of the Mark Twain Society and later wrote an appreciative introduction to *Pudd'nhead Wilson* in 1959, Langston Hughes left no recorded statement of deliberate emulation of Twain, nor was he subjected to the burden of a reviewer's predictions or appraisals of him in those terms as Lardner had seen. Not that he could have ever been pegged by a critic, anyway. His talents were too various and his achievements too diverse to lend themselves to easy identification.

Hughes wrote plays, poems and songs, autobiography and history, translations, travel literature and fiction, children's verse and stories, serious criticism and journalism. He even tried his hand at opera, and at one time contemplated collaborating on a "cantata" or a "composition with orchestra, singers, and perhaps a Narrator, perhaps to be

---

1941: I, Too, Sing America (New York: Oxford University Press, 1986), 19, Hughes was so "thrilled" by a reading of *Adventures of Huckleberry Finn* that he became a lifelong admirer of Twain.

35. Given the general tendency of the argument of this essay, I hope it goes without saying that I do not mean to examine the intricate and controversial response of African-American readers and writers to *Huckleberry Finn*. It should be apparent that I am more interested here in the broadly humanistic vernacular vision embodied in Hughes's Simple sketches than in whether or not *Huck Finn* is a racist book. Those interested in this latter question will find instructive James S. Leonard, Thomas A. Tenney, and Thadious M. Davis, eds., *Satire or Evasion? Black Perspectives on "Huckleberry Finn"* (Durham: Duke University Press, 1992). Arnold Rampersad's "*Adventures of Huckleberry Finn* and Afro-American Literature" particularly deals with Twain and his influence upon African-American writers.

36. Quoted in Arnold Rampersad, *The Life of Langston Hughes,* vol. 2, *1941–1967: I Dream a World* (New York: Oxford University Press, 1988), 223.

called MISSOURI after my native state. . . . It could have history in
it, and Mark Twain, and the rivers, and a bit of folk lore."[37] Like
Twain, too, Langston Hughes was an avid student of American humor. As if in answer to the volume *Mark Twain's Library of Humor,*
Hughes published an anthology called *The Book of Negro Humor.* The
prefatory note to this collection is pointedly unfunny and offhand-
edly personal and revealing:

> Humor is laughing at what you haven't got when you ought to have
> it. Of course, you laugh by proxy. You're really laughing at the other
> guy's lacks, not your own. That's what makes it funny—the fact
> that you don't know you are laughing at yourself. Humor is when
> the joke is on you but hits the other fellow first—before it boomer-
> angs. Humor is what you wish in your secret heart were not funny,
> but it is, and you must laugh. Humor is your own unconscious
> therapy.[38]

How unconscious the therapy of writing the Jesse Semple sketches
was for Hughes is uncertain. He once remarked that Simple "is just
myself talking to me. Or else me talking to myself."[39] Arnold Rampersad speculates that through the interplay between Boyd (a thinly
veiled version of Hughes himself) and Jesse Semple (the plainspoken
figure whose lack of restraint and simple vitality Hughes envied),
Hughes's comic sketches continually play about the edges of the author's subterranean fears and desires.[40] Whatever the nature of the
author's compelling interest in the figure of Jesse Semple and the dramatic opportunities he provided, it was sufficient stimulus to carry
him through two decades and more than 150 Simple sketches
published in the Chicago *Defender* and the *New York Post,* ample
material for the four book-length collections that eventually would
be published.

For our purposes, however, it is enough to say that the origins of
the imagined character (his complaints, preoccupations, and enthusi-

37. Quoted in Rampersad, *Life of Langston Hughes* 2:253.
38. *The Book of Negro Humor* (New York: Dodd, Mead, and Co., 1966), vii.
39. Quoted in Rampersad, *Life of Langston Hughes* 2:64–65.
40. See ibid., 2:64–65.

asms) sprang from powerful internal initiatives within the author that ultimately had little to do with literary tradition or even artistic ambition. But we may recast these same private conflicts in public terms by recurring to Ralph Ellison's contemplation of the abandoned legacy of *Huckleberry Finn*. For Ellison's appraisal of the deficiencies of modern American fiction, when measured against the achievement of *Huck Finn*, is answered in the example of the Simple sketches.

Mark Twain's portrayal of Jim, according to Ellison, avoided the stereotyped characterizations that came all too naturally to later writers. Jim is never idealized but is "drawn in all his ignorance and superstition, with his good traits and his bad. He, like all men, is ambiguous, limited in circumstance but not in possibility." Yet at the same time, and largely through Huck's relation to him, Jim is a potent symbol as well, not merely of the Negro but "as a symbol of Man." Huck's own adolescent and slow-dawning recognition of Jim's humanity simultaneously clarifies for the reader the relation Huck must sooner or later bear toward the existing social order and yet makes tangible and vivid his resistance to that same community.[41]

---

41. "Twentieth-Century Fiction and the Black Mask of Humanity," 48–49. Ellison never says so explicitly, but the whole thrust of his essay clearly implies that the terms of Huck's conflict are to be abstracted from the ingredients of a child's experience and in no way depend on the boy's self-conscious comprehension of his situation. The whole artistic and historical justification of Huck's "adolescence," Ellison observes, is that Twain was "depicting a transitional period" in American life and that, correspondingly, adolescence is "the time of the 'great confusion' during which both individuals and nations flounder between accepting and rejecting the responsibilities of adulthood" (50). If Huck actively and knowingly chose to perform a noble moral act, as some critics never tire of insisting he does do, the moral "message" of the book would be unmistakable, and readers would never have been able to consign the novel to the interests of a "boy's book." By the same token, however, the novel would have lost all its moral and humanizing force, since Huck would have embraced generalized and idealized fraternal values instead of responding to a felt attachment to Jim as an individual. If this were so, and since no "civilization" ever really denies its support of these values in the abstract, one might say that Huck's "problem" was solved, socially and politically, with the Emancipation Proclamation. But Twain knew, and Ellison knows, that the full and continuing interest of Huck's decision to go to hell and to help Jim has nothing to do with helping a race or advancing a political agenda but with preferring a known reality

For Huck, like Jim, serves a double function in the novel. In his relation to the river and to Jim, Huck is a humanist; in his relation to the larger social community, he is an individualist. Thus, Huck "embodies the two major conflicting drives operating in nineteenth-century America. And if humanism is man's basic attitude toward a social order which he accepts, and individualism his basic attitude toward one he rejects, one might say that Twain, by allowing these two attitudes to argue dialectically in his work of art, was as highly moral an artist as he was a believer in democracy, and vice versa."[42] Langston Hughes, however, combined in a single figure the functions Twain had distributed between Jim and Huck, and he named him Jesse B. Semple.

It is a critical commonplace to observe that Simple is an Everyman figure. His originality as a character derives almost entirely from Hughes's confident resistance of freakish literary excess and dramatic effect. Simple is compellingly ordinary, and the achievement is a rarity. "In all of Negro fiction," wrote Blyden Jackson in 1968, "the Negro who is unabashedly and simply an *average man* is as rare as once, in that same fiction, octoroons were disturbingly numerous."[43] There is nothing conciliatory in the averageness of Simple, however. His sometimes fantastic flights of imagination, his concocted dramas of revenge, his hep prayers for reconciliation are underwritten by a seemingly incurable sanity and hope.

Jesse Semple rants, raves, grumbles, and complains, but he invariably lands upon his moral and emotional feet. He imagines a righteous catastrophe, but he settles for a beer. In "Simple Prays a Prayer," Jesse takes as the text for an impromptu sermon Jesus' commandment to love one another. "I know the Bible, too," he insists:

(Jim) over an abstract penalty (hell). Or, as Willa Cather said of Thomas Mann's historical novels, *Huckleberry Finn* deals with a figure who "chooses," not with one who, rightly or wrongly, "chose." Huck's decision is revitalized with every reading precisely because, in its dramatic essentials, it is preideological and prepolitical.

42. Ibid., 50–51.

43. "A Word about Simple," reprinted in *Langston Hughes, Black Genius: A Critical Evaluation,* ed. Therman B. O'Daniel (New York: William Morrow and Co., 1971), 116.

"My Aunt Lucy read it to me. She read how He drove the money-changers out of the Temple. Also how He changed the loaves and fishes into many and fed the poor—which made the rulers in their high places mad because they didn't want the poor to eat. Well, when Christ comes back this time, I hope He comes back *mad* His own self. I hope He drives the Jim Crowers out of their high places, every living last one of them from Washington to Texas! I hope he smites white folks down!"

"You don't mean *all* white folks, do you?"

"No," said Simple. "I hope He lets Mrs. Roosevelt alone."[44]

What begins in frustration and anger ends in comic charity. In the end, Simple does not speak out of personal despair. Momentarily convinced by his own rhetoric, he speaks instead from an invented position of power. His prayer, if only in the imagination, serves as incantation and enacts an angry second coming that has the whole force of Christian dogma behind it. It is Simple's mercy, however, not God's, that spares Mrs. Roosevelt. In that quick double movement, Hughes supplies his vernacular hero with a common humanity, both as the indignant victim of a real society he inhabits and condemns (an individualist, in Ellison's terms) and a full partner in the community he imagines (a humanist).

This is humor in the subjunctive mood, and it is pervasive in the Simple sketches. In "High Bed," Simple imagines the freedom of a rocket ship: "I sure would rock so far away from this color line in the U.S.A., till it wouldn't be funny. I might even build me a garage on Mars and a mansion on Venus."[45] In "Confused" Jesse confides that he loves being black but likewise knows that in racist America he is marked for life. In one of his quick-tempo poetic riffs he defines his condition: "I am a Son of Ham from down in 'Bam and there ain't none other like I am. Solid black from front to back! And one thing sure—it won't fade Jack!"[46] In a single gesture, Simple asserts both his unique individuality and his solidarity with the black community and against the prevailing social oppression of African-Americans.

44. In *The Best of Simple* (1961) (New York: Hill and Wang, 1988), 10.
45. In ibid., 57.
46. In *Simple Speaks His Mind* (New York: Simon and Schuster, 1950), 173–74.

Unlike the Irishman or the Jew, a change of name will never change his social identity. But if it could and he desired to pass for white, Simple would take the name Patrick McGuire:

> "If I was going to pass for white, I might as well pass good. With an Irish name, I could be Mayor of New York."
> "A fine Mayor you would make."
> "A fine Mayor is right," said Simple proudly. "I would immediately issue a decree right away."
> "To what effect?"
> "To the effect that any colored man who wants to rent an apartment downtown can rent one and no landlord can tell him, 'We do not rent to colored.'"[47]

Boyd has trapped his friend, however, for he reminds him that as Patrick McGuire, Simple is no longer black. And he confuses Jesse still further by asking, "However, if you were white, sir, listen—would you want your daughter to marry a Negro?" "If my daughter didn't have no better sense," is his reply. But Simple knows that the question of intermarriage is always brought in to confuse the issue and is quick to remind his friend that, in point of fact, he doesn't have a daughter, he is not white, and even if he did have a daughter, she would not be white since he himself would simply be passing for white:

> "We was having a nice simple argument and you had to confuse the issue. Buy me a beer."
> "You drink too much," I said.
> "Please don't confuse *another* issue," said Simple.[48]

"Radioactive Redcaps" is yet another fantasy of empowerment. Simple imagines an atomic bomb falling in Harlem and that he has become "atomized." Once "charged," he fancies, he will "take charge." He would be able to set off a chain reaction, and "I am getting my chain ready now." By simply calling up his former landlady on the

47. "Confused," in ibid., 174.
48. Ibid., 175

telephone, he will be able to atomize her like a "Japanese tuna." Why, asks Boyd, do you think you will be able to survive an atomic explosion? His answer is to the point: "If Negroes can survive white folks in Mississippi," said Simple, "we can survive anything."[49]

Simple's circumstances are comically curious, but they are unremarkable. Though he typically speaks in or around Paddy's Bar in Harlem, he has traveled up north from Virginia, with a stopover in Baltimore (enough time to make a bad marriage with Isabel, who refuses to pay for their divorce). On Harlem streets, Simple cadges a beer from Boyd and literally talks his life. Sometimes, he reports to Boyd, he cozies up to his "after-hours gal," Zarita; but he actively courts and, once his divorce comes through, eventually marries his fiancée, Joyce. He tries to set a good example for his distant cousin "F. D." (Franklin Delano Roosevelt Brown), who has come up north to be with him. He frets over his homely cousin Minnie, complains about his heartless landlady, and pokes fun at Joyce's social-climbing friend, Mrs. Sadie Maxwell-Reeves.

These are the ingredients of Simple's everyday life. They humanize his fictional existence, but they never eclipse the external pressures of the color line that threaten to crush or distort that same humanity. Boyd believes his friend reduces everything to the race issue. "Your semantics makes things too simple," he says. Jesse's reply is as direct as it is comically outrageous:

> "Whatever you are talking about with your *see-antics,* Jack, at my age a man gets tired of the same kind of eggs each and every day— just like you get tired of the race problem. I would like to have an egg some morning that tastes like a pork chop."
> "In that case, why don't you have pork chops for breakfast instead of eggs?"
> "Because there is never no pork chops in my icebox in the morning."
> "There would be if you would put them there the night before."
> "No," said Simple, "I would eat them up the night before— which is always the trouble with the morning after—you have

49. In *Best of Simple,* 212, 213.

practically nothing left from the night before—except the race problem."[50]

By turns, Simple is cantankerous, magnanimous, shrewd, discouraged, gentle, ferocious, and generous, which is to say he is an unevenly average man. By turns, too, he is Huck Finn and Jim. Like Huck, people are constantly pecking on him, intent on improving and civilizing him. (Joyce one time tells him to hush and listen to an Italian libretto; Simple complains to his friend Boyd the next day, "I don't see why culture can't be in English.") And his resistance is sometimes as innocently evasive as Huck's; he too steps out at night (until the "A. M.," as Jesse is apt to say) to seek relief from custom and restraint. But, like Jim and unlike Huck, Simple desires admittance into and full partnership in the social order, not as it is, but as it ought to be.

It is both understandable and curious that Jesse Semple (and his creator) are so often regarded as out-of-date. Even in his own day, Hughes was accused of "backing into the future looking at the past."[51] But if there were ever a literary character who knows that politics is personal, it is Jesse Semple. Freedom means, among other, much more serious things, being able to gnaw a pork bone at your own front window. Joyce reports that this is simply not done and that Emily Post says "DON'T": "'Baby,' I says, 'Emily Post were white. Also, I expect, rich. That woman had plenty of time to gnaw her bones at the table. Me, I work.'"[52] Lack of freedom, on the other hand, means feeling the pain of restraint as acutely as the bunions on his feet. ("If anybody was to write the history of my life, they should start with my feet," he says in "Feet Live Their Own Life.")[53]

These sudden verbal incongruities and dislocations are the common stuff of humor, but Hughes has appropriated conventional comic devices and made them serve not only the uses of satire and comedy

50. "Two Sides Not Enough," in ibid., 214–16.
51. Owen Dodson, quoted in Richard Barksdale, *Langston Hughes: The Poet and His Critics* (Chicago: American Library Association, 1977), 87.
52. "Bones, Bombs, Chicken Necks," in *Best of Simple,* 200.
53. In ibid., 3.

but also the purpose of advancing a mature social vision. "With one exception," remarks Roger Rosenblatt in his elegant essay on Simple, "black literature has produced no full, self-sustaining humorous hero, either out of the desire to avoid reproducing end men, or because end men seem out of place in the depictions of a nightmare." And as he rightly observes, Jesse, like Huck, is a regionalist comic character, but, in a sense deeper and larger than geography, Simple's "region" is his blackness. Jesse Semple's dialect is the fundamental condition of his being, and he is eloquent. In structure, subject, and effect, Simple's casual talk has the quality of a streetwise, secular sermon. His vernacular speech is, to reemphasize Cox's distinction, a way of being, not a way of saying. And Rosenblatt makes explicit the connection between Twain and Hughes we have been contemplating in a general way: "Twain said he was always preaching when he wrote, that if humor emerged as part of the sermons, fine, but that he would have written the sermons in any case. . . . [Simple's] sermons are part of himself and so they are humorous naturally, but because like Twain he is first a moral man, then a humorist, we realize that amusement is not the most important reaction intended."[54]

What Hughes did intend, I believe, was to supply an image of an Everyman, who also happens to be black. Not that his blackness is incidental to the effect. Quite the contrary. Simple's personal experience—his deprivations, aggravations, and anger, as well as his hope, optimism, and resilience—mirror the condition and the welfare of the republic. Jesse Semple will never belong to Dubois's "talented tenth"; nor does he even begin to qualify as one of Harriet Beecher Stowe's "moral miracles." Still, in his own minor and ordinary way he is a miracle nonetheless. A democratic society can survive, even prosper, without a talented tenth (black or white), but it can never rise above the condition of the least of its well-meaning citizens, its Everyman or Everywoman. The final literary and moral effect of Jesse Semple is not that he is a potential enemy too dangerous to be ignored, but that he is a potential ally, too valuable to be neglected.

54. "The 'Negro Everyman' and His Humor," in *Veins of Humor,* ed. Harry Levin, 225–41, 235.

VI

By now it should be clear that the neglected legacy of *Huckleberry Finn* I have been attempting to identify as a vernacular vision is, in fact, a hopelessly old-fashioned liberal humanism, available equally to common readers, gifted writers, and, perhaps, even to literary critics. Twain banked on the approval of his "submerged clientele" (banked on them in a commercial as well as a moral sense), and the result was an image of the American author as a public man. He was, and is, the nation's funny fellow, but I doubt that even the most casually amused reader doesn't truly wish that Twain's humor were not funny.

Huckleberry Finn, Ántonia Shimerda, and Jesse B. Simple are vernacular moral heroes. They have suffered (though quite unequally) abuse, rejection, assault, and disenfranchisement, and they have survived. But that is not the foundation of their strength or the origin of our important interest in them. They are, it is true, wounded characters, but they are neither stronger for the hurt nor debilitated by the recollection of it. They are, we like to think, better than the conditions of their existence.

If modern American literature began with *Huckleberry Finn*, Huck (as a character and not a literary device) bears faint and uneven resemblance to so many of those figures of the imagination who claim a kinship with him. Huck Finn is often lonely, but he is never alienated. He is frequently petty, but seldom trivial. He is guilt ridden and self-deprecating, but he is never paralyzed by those feelings. Huckleberry Finn is nothing more than a fictional creation; and as decent a man as Mark Twain seems to have been, he was never so good as his created character. And as good as Huck is, he is not so very good; he is only better than he ought to be.

"Moral reform," says Thoreau, "is the effort to throw off sleep. . . . To be awake is to be alive. I have never yet met a man who was quite awake. How could I have looked him in the eye?" But, when Huck plays a trick on Jim, Jim not only looks Huck in the eye but scolds and humbles him, too. It is precisely in this dramatized moment that one feels that the moral inheritance which is a part of the legacy of

Huckleberry Finn will never degenerate into the sanctimonious or obscure. The example of Mark Twain involves writing about something, on behalf of some half-realized and dimly felt obligation not to the social order or to ideological prescription, but to the nagging impulsions of the imagination. The social responsibility of the novelist is always there, perhaps most importantly there when the author writes about something he or she cannot quite understand.

Perhaps it is fitting that a writer of our own day, who not so coincidentally wears his own white suit like a badge, should reintroduce in rather different terms the substance of Ellison's criticism of modern fiction. Tom Wolfe, in "Stalking the Billion-Footed Beast: A Literary Manifesto for the New Social Novel," argued for a reinvigorated social realism in American fiction. Judging from the number of responses and the degree of lively and angry interest this manifesto received, he touched a nerve in a way that Ellison's critique never did. Quite apart from the soundness of Wolfe's argument that contemporary writers have shied away from the provocative and inexhaustible literary opportunities that the "real" world throws in their way on an almost daily basis, Wolfe's reply to his several detractors is worth citing: "With very few exceptions, the towering achievements [in the novel] have taken the form of a detailed realism of the sort I am referring to. . . . And why? Because a perfectly sound and natural instinct told them that it is impossible to portray characters vividly, powerfully, convincingly, except as part of the society in which they find themselves."[55]

I am not at all certain that these same instincts prescribe a definite literary manner, the manner of Zola, Tolstoy, or Flaubert, for example. But they implicate the reader and the writer in contemplating the world not only as it is but as it might be. In "Prologues To What Is Possible," Wallace Stevens imagines an ordinary man on an extraordinary voyage:

55. Wolfe's essay appeared in *Harper's Magazine* (November 1989). The editors solicited responses from several novelists to the piece, and selections from those reactions appeared in the "Letters" section of the magazine in the February 1990 issue. Wolfe's response to his critics, from which the above quotation is taken, appeared in the March 1990 issue.

What self, for example, did he contain that had not yet been loosed,
Snarling in him for discovery as his attentions spread,
As if all his hereditary lights were suddenly increased
By an access of color, a new and unobserved, slight dithering,
The smallest lamp, which added its puissant flick, to which he gave
A name and privilege over the ordinary of his commonplace—
A flick which added to what was real and its vocabulary.[56]

This is a fragile and temporary hope, this puissant flick added to
the "ordinary of his commonplace." It may give rise to grand vernacular dreams and to the vocabulary of human possibility, but like all
dreams it may be dismissed with a flick of the wrist. In "Jazz, Jive,
and Jam," Jesse Semple relates his own plans for improving "interra-
cial meetings": "In my opinion, jazz, jive, and jam would be better
for race relations than all this high-flown gab, gaff, and gas orators
put out." If he had his way, he would liven things up with the music
of Duke Ellington or Count Basie. And he would offer to the meeting
his own resolution:

> "*Resolved:* that we solve the race problem! Strike up the band! Hit
> it men! Aw, play that thing! 'How High the Moon!' How high!
> Wheee-ee-e!."
> "What did Joyce say to that?" I demanded.
> "Joyce just thought I was high," said Simple.[57]

56. *The Collected Poems of Wallace Stevens* (New York: Alfred A. Knopf, 1968), 516–17.
57. *Best of Simple,* 242–43, 244–45.

IS *HUCKLEBERRY FINN* POLITICALLY CORRECT?

A S WITH SO MANY questions one may put to *Huckleberry Finn,* Twain has anticipated my topic here. The implicit contradiction of the author's "Notice" and his "Explanatory" is one of the several paradoxes of his book. The "Explanatory" insists upon a certain cultural diversity, and upon Twain's own meticulous and painstaking efforts to render several Mississippi River Valley dialects and thus to give voice to those who speak them. His characters (most of them disenfranchised in one way or another) are to speak for themselves, and we, his readers, are not to suppose that all these characters are trying to talk alike and not succeeding. So instructed, we may approach his heterogeneous narrative with impunity so long as we yield also to the unequivocal "Notice" that we not attempt to find motive, moral, or plot in it. What other novel has ever made such difficult claims upon the reader? We are to listen to its voices and resist (on pain of prosecution, banishment, or execution) even so slight a temptation to interpret this series of adventures as purposive or instructive or even useful. *Huckleberry Finn* thy tongue is diversity, thy authority is the long arm of the law, G. G., Chief of Ordnance.

I do not intend to answer the question my title poses. Indeed, I suspect that neither the book's most avid partisans nor its most vocal detractors would wish to deem *Huckleberry Finn* a politically correct novel. True, we are sometimes told that the novel is an "attack on racism" without ever being told, precisely, why we should believe it.

But by and large we prize *Huck* for its incorrectness; it is an incorruptibly incorrect book in nearly every particular. But the issues my title raises are delicate ones, and I hope you will indulge me if I approach the subject with a certain eager wariness and stalk it in a roundabout way. What I hope to offer in return for this indulgence is not, I hasten to add, a new reading of *Huckleberry Finn*. God forbid. Still less do I mean to infuse the novel with an ideological perspective. Quite the reverse. I hope to show that ultimately *Huckleberry Finn* resists, in fact refuses, ideology itself.

About a dozen years ago, Leslie Fiedler came to my campus to deliver a lecture. I can't recall the title, but I do recall that he observed that the customary Anglo-American response to the Klansmen's revenge scene in D. W. Griffith's *Birth of a Nation* is disturbingly positive, and that this fact testifies to the deep and abiding racist character of our culture. I am ashamed to say that I have never seen *Birth of a Nation* and therefore do not know what my own reaction to this controversial scene might be. But I have seen a few movies in my time.

As a child I used to go to the Westerns every Saturday afternoon. I grew up in a rather unique community called McNary, Arizona. It was a company lumber town and had originally been McNary, Louisiana. But when the yellow pine of Louisiana played out around the turn of the century, old man McNary picked up his town lock, stock, and barrel and moved it to ponderosa pine country, smack dab in the middle of the White Mountain Apache Reservation. It was a town of about four hundred souls. We, that is the families of the white company men, lived on the hill; the Chicano families lived just to the north of us, almost in the forest; the Blacks lived down the hill in what was called the "Quarters"; the Apaches, of course, lived all around the town, but not in the town itself.

Despite these well-understood boundaries, all the kids converged at the movie house on Saturday afternoons. There were separate drinking fountains at the entrance, and the black kids had to sit in the balcony. (Most of us kids, brown and white alike, usually said that they "got to sit" in the balcony and begrudged them their good fortune.) At any rate, we watched the newsreel, and the Batman serial, and a couple of Westerns every Saturday. At the age of four or five, I unthinkingly accepted, or rather never questioned, this segregated arrangement. On the other hand, every time the cavalry came to save the settlers from the Indians, which was every week, we all cheered; and I was sufficiently aware of race at that young age to ask my Native American friends why they, too, cheered for the cavalry and not the Indians. The explanation was irrefutable: "Those aren't Apaches; they're Navajos."

I put this anecdote up against Mr. Fiedler's observation about the subterranean racist nature of American culture. The only point I wish to make is so simple that I am somewhat embarrassed to make it: Our response to works of the imagination has a great deal less to do with political or social realities as such than with an imaginative identification with heroism, courage, nobility, and so forth. We cheer for the good guys in white hats, not because they and their hats are white, nor, for that matter, because they are guys, but because everything within the fictional world they inhabit marks them as good.

Identification, I confess, is a flimsy basis upon which to build any convincing reply to those who find *Huckleberry Finn* a racist book.[1] Ralph Ellison once confessed that when he read the novel, he identified with Huck, not Jim, and justified this natural response by observing that the Negro is likewise heir to "the human experience which is literature, and this might well be more important to him than his living folk tradition."[2] Now, I am not so benighted that I do

1. The whole process of identification is a mysterious one. One thing we may say about it, though, is that however fully one's emotional and moral states tally with those of a created character, there is always a critical faculty at work in the process of reading. No reader, no matter how naive, I think, ever took *Huckleberry Finn* as a literal recipe for moral heroism. If this were so, there would be hundreds of fourteen-year-old white boys searching out and linking their fortunes with black adult male fugitives. Nor, I suppose, has any young woman reader decided, after reading *The Scarlet Letter,* that the path to moral greatness is to marry an older man, have an adulterous relation with her minister, get pregnant, keep the baby, and linger in a contemptuous community. If this were the practical result of imaginative engagement, there really would be a hue and cry from white America to ban both novels.

2. "Twentieth-Century Fiction and the Black Mask of Humanity," in *Shadow and Act* (New York: New American Library, 1966), 72–73.

not know that Ellison is much out of favor these days—one thing that Jerry Falwell and Terry Eagleton can agree upon is the danger and evil associated with anything that passes for humanism. We live in an era of linguistic naturalism, which is to say that prevailing critical ideology has it that we no longer think our language, our language rather thinks us. Values, literary or other, are thus vanities, and discussing, adopting, or pursuing them is utter foolishness.

It is in this context that we might consider for a moment Shelley Fisher Fishkin's recent book, *Was Huck Black? Mark Twain and African-American Voices* (1993). Her argument runs something like this: African-American voices are fully integrated, at the level of discourse, into the text of *Huckleberry Finn* and are detectable in the speech of the novel's hero and narrator, Huck. Specifically, she argues that Mark Twain, from his youth, was alert to the cadences, syntax, and richness of metaphor of African-American dialect; he may even have learned from a slave named "Jerry" the satirical strategies, the rhetorical play, and the artful indirection known as "signifying." Many years later, Twain met a young black boy he dubbed "Sociable Jimmy" and published a piece under that title in the *New York Times* on November 29, 1874. Twain was so struck by the child that, apparently unconsciously, he allowed Sociable Jimmy's dialect to enter into the very texture of Huck's voice when he began to write *Huckleberry Finn* a year and a half later. In other words, what Neil Schmitz has called "Huckspeech" also happens to be, at least in part, "blackspeech."

Fishkin's research into her subject is comprehensive, and her documentation is ample. At times, however, her argument veers toward question begging—the tentative speculations of one paragraph become assertions of fact in the next. Still, one cannot fail to appreciate her motives or the rhetorical energy of her interests and commitments. Her title is provocative, but her conclusion claims eager assent:

> The research presented in this book suggests that *Huckleberry Finn* may be more subversive, ultimately, than we may have suspected. For Twain's imaginative blending of black voices with white ones (whether conscious or unconscious) effectively deconstructs "race" as a meaningful category. "Race," for Mark Twain, far from being the "ultimate trope of difference," was often simply irrelevant. The

problem of racism, on the other hand, was for Twain, and con-
tinues to be for us, undeniably real.[3]

I appreciate Fishkin's democratic impulses and admire her conclusions even if I am not fully convinced by her argument. But I worry
about what may be the ultimate effects and unintended by-products
of her emphasis upon Huck's language to the virtual exclusion of his
"adventures."

It is no secret that *Huckleberry Finn* is a very controversial book
these days, and the mere suggestion that Huck was to some degree
patterned after an African-American boy is likely to be embraced as
an idea congenial to those who like the novel but feel somewhat
uncomfortable in their admiration. For this notion may obviate many
of the difficulties teachers face when they start to discuss an American classic narrated by the son of Pap Finn and in which the word
nigger appears over 150 times. For others, the assertion may prove
appealing because it advances notions of multicultural education
without damaging the exalted status Mark Twain and his book have
enjoyed for several generations. This is a no-lose situation—*Huckleberry Finn* not only stays in the "canon" but belongs there, though for
rather different reasons than we previously supposed. Mark Twain
remains a public institution worthy of our admiration, and Huckleberry Finn is no longer an unself-conscious moral hero, but a construction of many American voices and therefore perhaps not moral
at all but at least politically correct.

Mark Twain enjoys a unique position among American authors.
He is not merely popular; he is a public institution and a public
property. No matter how much academics would like to have it
otherwise, our views about the man and his works will always be in
some measure answerable to and modified by the interests and attitudes of an unnumbered host of nonspecialist readers. For my part, I
believe this is a wholesome and fruitful relation. Fishkin's thesis
commands our interest because it concerns Mark Twain. Had it been

3. *Was Huck Black? Mark Twain and African-American Voices* (New York: Oxford
University Press, 1993), 144. The quoted expression "ultimate trope of difference" is
from Henry Louis Gates.

applied to George Washington Cable or Harriet Beecher Stowe, it likely would have gone unnoticed.

Somehow our attitude toward Twain and *Huckleberry Finn* matters—matters as a response to a cultural property, to be sure, but it matters as well because the novel challenges our tepid commitments and false assurances and promotes values we do not as yet own. "Race" may not be a meaningful linguistic category, but, as Fishkin rightly observes, racism is as real as it ever was. I publicly hope, but privately doubt, that acceptance of the fact that the American language is a rich compound of many voices and that our most famous vernacular novel might be an admixture of these voices will serve as something more than a social and moral palliative. I fear, however, that the prevailing logic of linguistic naturalism is ill suited to sponsor the small and spontaneous acts of human freedom Huck and Jim perform or the moral impulsions that give them dramatic force. At best, it can give but notional assent to truths and values that, if they are to mean anything at all, must finally be validated by our acts.

Long before postmodernists addressed the problem of culture, John Dewey had observed in *Freedom and Culture* (1939) that definitions of human nature and culture are instruments of coercion and control. Democracy and human freedom rely far less upon pious proclamations, ingenious hypotheses, and rationally crafted social structures than they do upon constantly renewable commitments: "Anything that obscures the fundamentally moral nature of the social problem is harmful, no matter whether it proceeds from the side of physical or psychological theory. Any doctrine that eliminates or even obscures the function of choice of values and enlistment of desires and emotions in behalf of those chosen weakens personal responsibility for judgment and for action."[4] I seriously hope that awareness of African-American elements in Huck's speech will not obscure the fact that, in terms of the fiction, he is a white boy struggling, quite unevenly, with some pretty nasty extralinguistic problems that he only dimly comprehends. For Jim is Huck's "problem," and he was apparently Mark Twain's problem as well.

4. *Freedom and Culture* (New York: Capricorn Books, 1963), 172.

"Sociable Jimmy," like "A True Story," is a sketch mostly narrated in black dialect, a transcription of an event witnessed and a voice heard, not the creation of a rounded human being fully imagined. For both these sketches, Twain relied upon a good ear and a faithful memory. "A True Story" was written ("Repeated Word for Word as I Heard It" he reminds us) the morning after Clemens heard Mary Cord, the original for "Aunt Rachel," tell her story on the porch at Quarry Farm. Of Sociable Jimmy he says, "I took down what he had to say, just as he said it—without altering a word or adding one." But Twain's working notes for *Huckleberry Finn* indicate that Jim's dialect did not come so easily. Why then did Clemens have trouble rendering Jim's dialect? My guess is that Twain found it rather easier to transcribe African-American voices than to imagine African-Americans as fully human. The fact that he even tried (however disappointing, even obnoxious, the result is for some readers) is noteworthy. That Twain sometimes chose to speak his own mature convictions through Jim instead of Huck is remarkable. That he sometimes allowed Jim to speak for himself is incredible.

Perhaps it is worth noting that on the same page of the *New York Times* that printed "Sociable Jimmy" there appeared a brief column entitled "The Kentucky Kuklux." The article is merely the reprinting of a proclamation issued by Governor Preston Leslie of Kentucky offering a reward for several Klansmen. It reads, in part:

> On the night of the 27th of October, 1874, a body of masked and disguised men, numbering twenty to twenty-five, did unlawfully enter the private residence of one Jos. Terry, colored, in the County of Todd, shot at him a number of times, and robbed his house; that on the same night they unlawfully entered the house of one Mack Jessup, of color, and robbed him of a gun; . . . that on the night of the 20th day of August last, said body of masked and disguised men visited the said house of Mat Link again, forced her to travel with them three miles, and show them where her husband was. They then shot and wounded him, and killed a colored boy named Christian, and afterward, the same night killed her said husband.

I do not know whether Governor Leslie was successful in bringing this gang to justice. I do know that through the resources of Twain's art the voices and figures of Sociable Jimmy, Aunt Rachel, and Jim are available to us. The voice of a black boy named Christian is not. His death, whatever else one may want to say about it, is a moral outrage. He belongs in the company of Emmett Till, Rodney King, and so many others. And in the face of such realities, fiction cannot do very much except in its own small way help us to perceive that they are, in fact, offensive beyond belief.

Perhaps some shift in our linguistic and conceptual paradigms will, one day, have its benevolent effects upon the state of the union. Nevertheless, I can sympathize with a fiction writer interviewed on National Public Radio some time ago. He had written a short story about a marriage breaking up. The husband, a fireman, was a callous clod, and the story was meant to dramatize his unthinking cruelty. The author, a few months after the story was published, received a letter from a firefighters' organization demanding a public apology for so maligning the character of firemen. Literature, the author complained, is in the process of being paradigmed to death, and this writer was both amused and annoyed to discover that he had written so politically incorrect a story.

The problem, of course, is not with reading but with interpretation, though, again, prevailing critical opinion has all but collapsed this distinction. For the last ten or fifteen years I have taught Willa Cather's *O Pioneers!* as often as I could, and I have noticed that none of my white male students has any difficulty whatsoever identifying with Alexandra Bergson, not only as the hero of that novel, but as the mythic embodiment of an American pioneering spirit that is unquestionably female. Some, however, do balk when I point out that by implication that same figure repudiates such time-honored assumptions as that the history of America is the history of rugged individuals preserving the force of personality by escape to the frontier, or that the East represents the Past, and the West, the Future. For *O Pioneers!* calls both these assumptions, and many others as well, into question.

Huckleberry Finn has always been something of a subversive book. In the beginning it was banned because it encouraged mischief in

America's youth. I have heard that it was for a time banned in China because it undermined a culture devoted to ancestor worship—Huck does not display a proper reverence for his father. Then there is the apocryphal story that a public librarian removed the novel from the shelves because of the homosexual elements in it—and I can imagine Leslie Fiedler, if he ever heard this story, saying, "That's not what I meant at all." The trouble, as I say, is with interpretation, not with reading.

The more recent banning of *Huckleberry Finn* on the basis of the rendering of Jim as an unflattering portrait of a black man, on the one hand, and the excessive, perhaps obsessive use of the word *nigger* on the other, is a far more serious charge, but not because previous critiques were incidental, even superficial complaints. If, indeed, *Huckleberry Finn* was in any way subversive to late Victorian American culture or to the whole notion of a republic of virtue populated and ruled by slightly overgrown Good Boys routing out and punishing Bad Boys, it was subversive indeed. If, for the Chinese, Huck's cagey defiance of the father discredited a politically altered but still lively sense of ancestor worship, he is, in fact, a dangerous character. What makes the charge of racism far more serious is that, if true, it serves to damn all those (mostly white male) critics who have for decades defended the book, if not as a potently antiracist book, at least as a profoundly moral one. Moreover, unlike the other charges, this one unsettles our conviction about what Twain was trying to do in his novel. (Twain meant to disturb the prevailing American ethos; he meant nothing at all about China or the Chinese; and he meant and probably thought he had effectively damned race prejudice.) In contemplating the political correctness of *Huckleberry Finn,* we are willy-nilly caught up in such questions as: What is the relation of the author to his or her book? What is the social function of literature? Is the canonical status of this novel evidence of cultural hegemony and racist myopia?

And insofar as we appropriate our past and make it serve the uses of our present, the question of *Huckleberry Finn* becomes a very simple one, expressed in the obnoxious vernacular of our own day: Do we want a book that makes Anglo-Americans feel bad about themselves, or one that makes African-Americans feel good about themselves? The questions have an inevitable corollary: Is literature in some way humanistic in the sense that it presupposes the possibility of moral vision and an attendant willingness to "do the right thing?" Or is it rather a signifying chain that somehow thinks us and therefore, in the interests of certain political objectives, must be condemned or, more likely, construed in such a way that (through the auspices of an instructed vision that we may call criticism) alters not the understanding but the structure of thought itself.

Now, whites have been feeling bad about themselves for centuries; in fact, I rather suspect that we enjoy feeling bad about ourselves and are sometimes inclined to designate the more effective forms of this self-torture "The Arts." Coincidentally, I was recently serving on a college committee with the peculiar title "The Ethnic Civility Task Force." This moral SWAT team was comprised of several diverse and well-meaning sorts, but I must confess that I became tired of hearing my white colleagues say, "Hey, I'm a sensitive guy!" One of the black members put his finger on the problem when he observed that "sensitivity" has its own mysterious logic to it: "Pretty soon, we'll have to be sensitive to the needs of left-handed people, and bald-headed people, and clumsy people, and blacks will be put on the back burner once again."[5]

I can recall my own most embarrassing moment of sensitivity. I was teaching a composition course to a group of Navajo women many years ago. I determined to be relevant, and one day I brought copies of the Navajo Night Chant for discussion. But discussion was not forthcoming; instead there was whispering and muttering among the students. "Did I do something wrong?" I asked. "No," they as-

---

5. Not long ago an editorial writer in *Time* sardonically remarked that perhaps we ought refer to short people as the "vertically challenged." By extension, I suppose, we ought call tall people "vertically gifted." And one of the most absurd instances I can recall is the objection of a school board to the use of the word *bitch* in one of Laura Ingalls Wilder's Little House novels. In the novel the word is applied not to a woman (which might be cause for complaint) but to a female dog. Sever the relation between signifier and signified and introduce sensitivity to fill the vacancy, and our language can think us in peculiar directions, it seems.

sured me. "But that song is sacred to us." "Oh, then I shouldn't talk about it?" "Oh you can talk about it all you want to," they insisted. "But we can't listen to you."

And the fictional epitome of sensitivity, I suppose, is Bigger Thomas's lawyer, Boris Max. *Native Son* was of course hailed as a powerful indictment of white racist culture, and so it is. However, my sampling of reviews of the novel in African-American periodicals does not square with the standard reaction of white readers and reviewers. For many blacks, Max, his political commitments and sensitivity notwithstanding, was just another white man giving a black man the runaround.

As Kenneth Burke once observed, capitalist societies, stressing as they do the individual, nevertheless achieve some degree of social cohesion by two antithetical means—war and charity. Both, of course, excite and promote feelings of superiority, racial and other. Our devastation of Iraq brings us together, and our contribution to the United Way brings us together. Sensitivity, it seems to me, is but a noninstitutionalized form of charity, or worse, pity; and it is as welcome an ally in institutions of political correction as it is in our so-called kinder and gentler republic.

As a critical principle, at any rate, it is chaotic and pernicious. One can, indeed some readers do, feel pity for each and every character in *Huckleberry Finn*—Pap because he hasn't a decent pair of shoes; Huck because he was pestered by the Widow and abused by his father; the Wilks girls; the Shepherdsons; the Grangerfords; the drunken Boggs; the well-meaning, God-fearing Silas Phelps; even the king and the duke. The sensitive guy who reads this book is apt to be paralyzed by the superabundance of his good and charitable feelings.

Now, and here at last I begin to move in on the subject at hand, Twain presented in Huck and Jim twin images of nobility, images contrary to what he knew or thought he knew about the ways of the world and of human possibility. Whatever else they may be, Huck and Jim were for their author metaphors, metaphors of their own human possibilities, nothing more, and certainly nothing less. And Twain wished to believe in them. The desire to believe in a metaphor, observed Wallace Stevens, "is to stick to the nicer knowledge of / Belief, that what it believes in is not true."[6] Of course we know, and I'd hazard that Twain did as well, that Huck and Jim are not true—it was more realistic, even probable, that Jim should have gotten lynched or that Huck would have turned Jim in than otherwise.

Actually, I am little interested in protecting Twain from the charge of racial prejudice. By nearly any reckoning Samuel Clemens was something of a racist, though the form it took was typically paternalistic rather than actively prejudicial. However, I might extenuate this charge by claiming that the imaginative self who created *Huckleberry Finn* ought not be confused with the ordinary self who, on the one hand, wrote abundant racist remarks in letters to his mother, or, on the other, paid a black man's tuition to Yale. The question of whether or not Samuel Clemens was a racist seems to me urgently, even crucially unimportant. I am far more interested in protecting Twain from the charge of being a sensitive guy.

And the record of Twain's strivings with his novel indicate that his manifold purposes and accidental effects fall away as Jim nudges his way to the center of the novel's concerns. Jim refuses to be put on the back burner, and it is Twain's imaginative, not his political courage that, by allowing to Jim speak for himself, finally claims our admiration.[7] We become less and less interested in the anti-Southern, antisentimental, antiaristocratic, anti-everything-under-the-sun elements in the novel, and more and more concerned with its affirmations, which is to say we become more and more concerned with Jim. Jim not as a representative of the Negro, the oppressed, or the wretched, but as Jim.

6. "The Pure Good of Theory," in *The Collected Poems of Wallace Stevens* (New York: Alfred A. Knopf, 1968), 332.

7. Twain's working notes for the novel show a preoccupying and continuing concern with Jim's dialect; they also reveal that the author had contemplated giving Jim an instant education, presumably with the intent of outfitting the runaway slave for a larger and more vocal role in the several conversations that take place particularly in the latter half of the book. Twain considered having Huck teach Jim to read and write, instruct him in history and even astronomy. See "Mark Twain's Working Notes" and "Mark Twain's Marginal Working Notes" in the California-Iowa edition of *Adventures of Huckleberry Finn,* ed. Walter Blair and Victor Fischer (Berkeley and Los Angeles: University of California Press, 1988), 711–64.

Two of the most conspicuous objects of Twain's satire are war (or organized violence) and charity (or sentimentality). But if one could magically subtract from the book all the instances of violence—not merely the feud chapters or the Boggs shooting but the proposed lynching of Sherburn or whatever happened to Pap on the floating house or even the desire to ransom the Sunday School girls to death; and then if one could take from the remainder all instances of charity (the slave hunters' forty dollar acquittal of their responsibility to Huck and his supposed father with smallpox, or the determination of the Judge to make a new man of Pap, or the Widow Douglas, who wishes to save Huck (the poor lost lamb!), or Emmeline Grangerford's insufferable odes)—if, as I say, one could perform this sort of higher mathematics, what would be left? Not much, I'd guess, but that "community of misfortune," Huck and Jim. And they, as outcasts and runaways, are happily exempt from the need for social cohesion.

Yet they are hardly pure. Twain's realism works by a kind of mean averaging of experience; or perhaps a more fashionable way of putting it is that it contains and announces its own ambiguities, it deconstructs itself before a critic lays a glove on it. *Huckleberry Finn* was a book motivated by multiple intentions, and it achieves diverse, even contradictory effects. Jim is a coward aboard the *Walter Scott* and a hero when Tom gets shot; he is alternately obsequious and insistent, curious and bullheaded, boastful and self-recriminating, credulous and shrewd.[8] As for Huck, I doubt that he is any more inconvenienced by the moral dilemma he faces in his desire to help Jim than he was by wearing starched collars or mumbling over his victuals. His decision to help Jim is as trivial and immediate as an itch that has to be scratched or a sneeze that has to be sneezed. And as for deciding to go to hell, we know from the very first page of the novel that he wasn't much interested in playing the harp anyway.

8. For Ralph Ellison, these same ambiguities are a tribute to Twain's moral vision, a quality he insists that moderns such as Hemingway, anxious to emulate Twain's technical improvisations, have been all but blind to: "Jim is drawn in all his ignorance and superstition, with his good traits and his bad. He, like all men, is ambiguous, limited in circumstance but not in possibility" ("Twentieth-Century Fiction and the Black Mask of Humanity," 48–49).

The beauty, the sheer magnificence of Huck's moral decision is how very small it is. Unlike his earlier decision to help Jim Turner aboard the *Walter Scott,* there is no sense of adventure in the prospect. Unlike his decision to help the Wilks girls, there is no pity in it. And despite his own fears, Huck is in no real danger of becoming a low-down abolitionist. He is absolutely incapable of abstracting from his own experience a general principle, and had he been allowed to reach his majority and thereby given to such generalizing, Huck would likely have become as shiftless as Pap, as indeed Twain predicted he would.

We know that the curious genesis of *Huckleberry Finn* introduced several textual peculiarities and ruptures. However, a far more serious rupture, it seems to me, occurs right after the raft is hit by the riverboat at the end of chapter 16.[9] When Huck surfaces he calls out for Jim "about a dozen times," but he never really worries about him. Instead, Huck climbs ashore and is soon involved in other adventures. For all Huck knows, Jim is dead or injured, but his creator had drifted from the so-called moral center of his book and was so eager to get to a satire of southern aristocratic pretension that he was for the moment no longer much interested in Jim or his flight.

By chapter 18 Huck and Jim are rejoined, however, and soon they are once more on the river. As much as Twain might have wanted to get shed of Jim, he couldn't. Jim unnecessarily complicated his plot, for not only was it absurd to have a slave escaping south, but the two had to travel at night to avoid the river communities. Jim's mere existence imposed all sorts of limitations on his author. After Jim's early appearance in the novel Twain seems to have pretty much forgotten about him. Yet Jim turns up again on Jackson's Island. The

9. Until the recent discovery of the first half of the *Huckleberry Finn* manuscript, it had been supposed that after he wrote this episode, Twain dropped the manuscript for some time and that when he returned to it he had other things on his mind than the comradeship of two outcasts. Now it appears that Twain's first burst of composition the summer of 1876 ran well into chapter 18. Nevertheless, it is clear that he was excited by the satirical possibilities of a southern feud and, even in so brief a time, may have altogether forgotten Jim until he revived the character at the end of chapter 18.

river might have drowned him, but he survives to repair the raft and wait for Huck. The working notes for the novel indicate the possibility that Twain contemplated having Jim lynched, but he missed every opportunity to do so.[10] The king and the duke sold him (to Abram Foster, they say) but Huck finds him again at the Phelps farm. Twain made a note to himself to *"Blow up* cabin," but he did not indicate whether Jim would be in it at the time.[11] And even after Twain had manufactured a conclusion to the novel and had set Jim free, the image of Jim still nagged at him, it seems. At any rate, Twain interpolated half of chapter 12 and all of chapters 13 and 14, chapters that dramatize Jim's native capacity to reason regarding Frenchmen who refuse to talk like men and his moral indignation at King Solomon as the sort of biblical patriarch who prefers the "bo'd'n house" of a million souls to sensible and dignified employment.

Even then Twain was not through with Jim (or perhaps it was the other way round). For he planned a lecture tour to make some cash and to promote the book, and when he sent proof sheets of his novel to his fellow lecturer, George Washington Cable, asking for suggestions about what he might read on the tour, Cable particularly recommended the "King Sollermun" episode and "How Come a Frenchman doan' Talk Like a Man" (a title Cable recommended over the needlessly offensive "You can't learn a nigger to argue").[12]

Jim stalked his creator. The author gave him his voice, but not even Mr. Mark Twain was going to shut him up. The novelist Fay Weldon makes the distinction between characters that are "described" and those that are "invented." When an author describes a character, she observes, all of the prejudices and prepossessions one has about the world and its people go into that character. But when an author invents a character, the character takes on its own life and speaks its

10. For the evidence for this supposition, see "'Learning a Nigger to Argue': Quitting *Huckleberry Finn*" above.

11. See the "Working Notes" C–9, page 755 of the California-Iowa edition of the novel.

12. See editorial comment in *Mark Twain and George W. Cable: The Record of a Literary Friendship,* ed. Arlin Turner (East Lansing: Michigan State University Press, 1960), 47.

own world.[13] Huck, virtually from the beginning, was an invented character. By degrees, Twain ceased to describe Jim and began to invent him.

Whether or not Twain the man was a racist (a charge that seems oddly superfluous in this context), his imaginative parts created a character who challenged Twain's own moral nature (or, more accurately, called it forth), just as he had Huck's. Houston Baker once observed that he made a living by telling people things they don't want to hear but that they know are true. This, I submit, was the method of Twain's realism in *Huckleberry Finn,* with the important difference that Twain was rendering truths, particularly in and through Jim, that perhaps he himself did not want to hear but that he knew were true. Uncharacteristically, Twain had the human decency to keep his mouth shut and listen, but he wisely knew that he might have to call in the Chief of Ordnance to have us do the same.

13. *Letters to Alice on First Reading Jane Austen* (New York: Carroll and Graf Publishers, 1984), 88.

Index

Ade, George, 120
Adventures of Augie March (Bellow), 110
Adventures of Huckleberry Finn (Twain): manuscript of, 2–6, 5n2, 12–13, 64, 98, 160n9; significance of Jim in, 7, 20–22, 33–34, 63–82 passim, 137–38, 154–55, 158–62; the problem of race in, 7, 66–67, 70–72, 75–77, 135n35, 147–48, 150–51, 155–56; working notes for, 12, 13–16, 26, 32–33, 66, 69, 81, 102, 158n7, 161; composition of, 12–38 passim, 65, 160n9; stages of composition of, 13–14, 15–16; as escapist novel, 18–25, 28; final stages of composition of, 16, 30–38, 62–68, 69–70; opening chapters of, 19–20, 98–100; Huckleberry Finn as satiric device in, 26–28, 35–37, 47, 95–96; as social satire, 26–31, 158–59; affirmations in, 34–35, 39–41, 158; Huckleberry Finn as character in, 35–36, 90–96; evasion chapters in, 36–37, 66–67, 102–3; conclusion of, 37–38, 63–65, 101; revisions of, 38, 39; narrative of, 39–40, 92, 97–104; Huckleberry Finn as narrator of, 54, 86–96 passim; realism of, 83–89, 100–103; as preideological novel, 89n5, 144–45, 137n41, 148, 157–60; influence upon later American writers, 112–19. *See also* Twain, Mark

Adventures of Tom Sawyer, The (Twain), 9, 18, 19, 20, 96, 99
"Alibi Ike" (Lardner), 121
Anderson, Sherwood, 110, 114, 118–19
"Art of Fiction, The" (James), 104
Atlantic Monthly, 46
Autobiography (Twain), 111

Baker, Houston, 162
Baldwin, James, 77
Barrie, James, 113
Basie, Count, 146
"Bear, The" (Faulkner), 110
Bell, Michael Davitt, 27, 84
Bellamy, Gladys, 98
Bellow, Saul, 110
Bergson, Henri, 1
Biglow Papers, The (Lowell), 110
Billy Budd, Sailor (Melville), 56, 60
Birth of a Nation (Griffith), 148
Blaine, James G., 55
Blair, Walter, 4–7, 14–18, 28, 36, 39, 44, 45, 50, 60, 68, 69, 73, 98, 109
Book of Negro Humor, The (Hughes), 136
Brooks, Van Wyck, 108
Bryant, William Jennings, 133
Budd, Louis J., 70, 106, 106n1
Bunyan, John, 129
Burke, Kenneth, 9, 22, 22n17, 157

Cable, George Washington, 38, 53, 55, 67, 72, 152, 161